Wilhelm von Bode, Rembrandt Harmenszoon van Rijn, C. (Cornelis) Hofstede de Groot, Florence Simmonds

The Complete Work Of Rembrandt

Wilhelm von Bode, Rembrandt Harmenszoon van Rijn, C. (Cornelis) Hofstede de Groot, Florence Simmonds

The Complete Work Of Rembrandt

ISBN/EAN: 9783741153389

Manufactured in Europe, USA, Canada, Australia, Japa

Cover: Foto ©Andreas Hilbeck / pixelio.de

Manufactured and distributed by brebook publishing software (www.brebook.com)

Wilhelm von Bode, Rembrandt Harmenszoon van Rijn, C. (Cornelis) Hofstede de Groot, Florence Simmonds

The Complete Work Of Rembrandt

THE COMPLETE WORK

OF

REMBRANDT

HISTORY, DESCRIPTION AND HELIOGRAPHIC REPRODUCTION

OF ALL THE MASTER'S PICTURES

WITH A STUDY OF HIS LIFE AND HIS ART

THE TEXT BY

WILHELM BODE

DIRECTOR OF THE ROYAL GALLERY, BERLIN

ASSISTED BY

C. HOFSTEDE DE GROOT

DIRECTOR OF THE PRINT ROOM, AMSTERDAM MUSEUM

FROM THE GERMAN BY FLORENCE SIMMONDS

FIRST VOLUME

PARIS

CHARLES SEDELMEYER, PUBLISHER

6, RUE DE LA ROCHEFOUCAULD, 6

1897

AUTHOR'S PREFACE

THE historic tendency of nineteenth century research has given a strong impetus to the worship of the great men of the past, and has thus stimulated the public desire to commemorate them by means of monuments. At no other period have so many bronze and marble statues been raised, not only to princes, generals, and statesmen, who have contributed to the development of national life, but to the men of art and science who are the glory and the boast of their country. For the great masters of the plastic arts, however, there can be, I think, no worthier memorial than the reproduction of their works with all possible fidelity and completeness, for by this means the greatness of their genius and the extent of their achievement may be best set forth for the recognition of posterity.

So far, no such monumental illustration of any great painter's art has been accomplished. The nearest approach to it was made with the works of Rubens. The result, however, was unsatisfactory, because, in spite of the support of the Belgian government, the process of reproduction employed was insufficient and defective. A set of reproductions from Albrecht Dürer's drawings is now in progress, which may certainly be cited as a model for such publications. The preliminary essays made with the work of Leonardo scarcely encourage us to hope for their completion for several decades.

In spite of the superabundance of material, and the absence of any kind of state-aid, more has been done for the work of Rembrandt than for that of any other master. This is, no doubt, because this master has gradually entered more and more into the sphere of universal interests throughout the second half of our nineteenth century. Many important books on his life and works have been published — by Smith, by Vosmaer, by Wurzbach and — last not least — by Emile Michel. Rembrandt's complete etched work has already been reproduced several times : by Charles Blanc, by E. Dutuit, and recently (perhaps indeed exhaustively) by Rovinski. A series of excellent fac-similes from the rich store of his drawings has been published under the direction of Dr. F. Lippmann. But a reproduction of his complete work as a painter has not yet been attempted.

The study of Rembrandt's works has been my favourite pursuit from my youth, and my official position has given me unusual facilities for the examination of those works, both in public and private collections. I have thus been able to collect a rich stock of material bearing upon the master, part of which I published in 1883, in my " Studien zur Geschichte der holländischen Malerei ". Shortly afterwards, I conceived the idea of a still more fascinating task — a complete survey of all

33

Rembrandt's pictures with their history, their detailed description, and above all, with their most perfect reproduction.

Many years passed, however, before I was able to carry out my scheme. In the first place, a successful rendering by means of photography was not to be thought of, until the isochromatic method came into use, and direct reproductions were made possible by the heliographic process. Even then, the undertaking seemed, to the publishers to whom I suggested it, almost impracticable; on the one hand, its costliness was a sufficient obstacle, while, on the other, they were confronted by the immense difficulty of procuring photographs from all Rembrandt's known pictures, over five hundred in number, scattered throughout the different countries of Europe and North America, the majority of them in private collections. The final realisation of my hopes is due to the happy circumstance of my finding in the well-known art-publisher, M. Charles Sedelmeyer, a courageous and disinterested coadjutor, who shared my enthusiasm for the master, more than a tithe of whose works has passed through his collection. Thanks to his active co-operation, all difficulties were overcome, and the carrying out of the great work on the most extensive scale, and by the most artistic means, was assured in a comparatively short time. It is most encouraging to find, from the number of subscriptions received, even before the issue of the first volume, that his efforts have been sympathetically recognised by the art-loving public.

I must farther gratefully acknowledge the cordial assistance I have received from the directors of public galleries, and the owners of private collections, who did their utmost to ensure the success of the photographs, which were executed by the first firms in Europe.

In cataloguing the works, I have chosen the chronological order as that which gives the scientific student the pleasure of following the master step by step in his development, and also as that best calculated to preserve the critic from over-subjective pronouncements. To facilitate reference to particular pictures, however, a short index will be added at the close of the work, in which the pictures will be classified according to their subjects, and their present domiciles.

The first seven volumes will contain heliogravures of all Rembrandt's known pictures, with their history, and their description. In each volume, the catalogue will be preceded by a critical analysis of the works there reproduced, and of the artist's development during the period illustrated. The eighth and last volume will contain a list of Rembrandt's etchings and drawings, and an illustrated catalogue of various lost works, known to us only by old engravings, but will consist in the main of the master's biography, and an appreciation of his artistic importance and individuality. Dr. Hofstede de Groot, who has given me valuable help in connection with the history and literature of the pictures, will contribute a series of documents bearing directly upon Rembrandt's life, or containing the judgments of contemporaries on his art.

Berlin, october 1, 1896.

WILHELM BODE.

INTRODUCTION

REMBRANDT'S YOUTHFUL WORKS

PERIOD OF ACTIVITY IN HIS NATIVE CITY, LEYDEN,
1627 TO 1631

HE juvenile works of an artist — and this is especially true of the greatest artists — as a rule, are only to be enjoyed and understood by those capable of judging them as part of an organic whole, and recognising the significance of their relation to his later development. He who can take pleasure only in the mature and perfect work of art — and here many artists and amateurs meet on common ground — is repelled by the unfamiliar elements, the evidences of the "prentice hand" more or less apparent in all such youthful essays, and finds himself entirely out of sympathy with them. In most cases he refuses to accept them as genuine, in spite of documents and proofs. To him, on the other hand, who looks upon art not merely as an isolated manifestation, but who follows its line of development, and studies it in its relation to the whole history of culture, there is a special interest over and above pure aesthetic pleasure, in considering it from the historic point of view, in the light of a knowledge of the development of schools as well as of individual artists. The youth of a master is peculiarly fascinating to all who study him on these lines. To trace his strivings after individual expression, his warfare with tradition and teaching, his delvings into the depths of Nature, and her powerful workings upon his fresh mind, is not only a process of deep psychologic interest, but the true basis for a just appreciation of the artist in his whole manifestation and significance.

There is, perhaps, no master who so strikingly illustrates all this as Rembrandt. In his juvenile works, which we can trace so far back as his twenty-first year, there is often much that is so incomplete, so extravagant, sometimes even so repellent, that the layman passes them by either with ridicule or indifference. On the other hand, they shew, even at this early period, such marked individuality, such a radical departure from established precedent, such a notable endeavour to give depth and force to the motive by an entirely new method of illumination, they betray such a passionate desire on the part of the youthful artist to go back to Nature, and discard the vicious methods of his teachers, that every work, no matter how trivial in scope and subject, has a deep interest for the student.

That the earliest efforts of the greatest of painters should consist, not of simple studies, portraits or sketches, but of set compositions, is a fact which finds its explanation in human nature itself. An attraction towards the vast and the visionary, a yearning after the highest, is one of the noblest and most characteristic traits of youth. Thus Rembrandt's earliest authenticated works, some eight or nine pictures painted in 1627 and 1628, are all compositions, and deal almost exclusively with subjects from the Old and New Testaments. There is a remarkable affinity between them all; they consist of one, or of two or three figures, laboriously painted from the model, and surrounded by a quantity of appropriate accessories, arranged in the same tentative fashion, and carefully studied from the originals. The small size of these works, the colour and the handling, the thinly painted brown shadows, and the loaded high lights, no less than the arrangement and installation, the costumes, and even to some extent the conception, betray the still dominant influence of his masters, Swanenburgh and Lastman. These masters, who in their own day ranked among the first artists of Holland, have scarcely more than a historic interest for us, and even this they owe mainly to their connection with their great pupil. Superficial and meticulous in their conception and treatment of the subject, inartistic in their colour, weak in their drawing, and lacking all delicacy in their perception of Nature, hard and often crude in the opposition of light and shadow, there was but one direction in which it was possible for them to influence their pupil favourably : this was in their preference for deep and solemn themes, such as appeal strongly to Protestant sympathies, and their simple, intimate, almost genre-like conception and treatment of scriptural motives. The art of these masters, mediocre as it was, undoubtedly stimulated, and even to some extent inspired Rembrandt's genius. The themes they loved sank deeply into his spirit; he learned to make the expression of the spiritual life his chief concern, even in the treatment of the trivial and the disconnected; and more gifted artists of like tendencies, such as Elsheimer and Bramer, influenced him in the same sense, and helped him to continue his way steadily towards the chosen goal.

The earliest date we find on any work by Rembrandt is 1627, which appears on two pictures. Very diverse in subject, there is a close affinity between them in appearance and execution. One is the *Money-Changer* in the Berlin Gallery (Plate 1), the other the *St. Paul in Prison* of the Stuttgart Gallery (Plate 2). In the one we have the solitary figure of an old man, who tests a coin by the light of a candle, surrounded by a confusion of ledgers, money-bags, and other such accessories; in the other, a venerable, bearded man, seated among his books, and meditating deeply over the letter before him; a sword hangs on the wall by his side, and a ray of sunlight strikes full upon him. In both these pictures, the painter still relies almost slavishly on the model; both have the weaknesses of inexperience: careful and laboured in handling, they are dry and cold in colour, and hard in the exaggerated opposition of light and shadow. In his rendering of the scene, the young painter produces a certain superficial effect, and fails to express the inward emotion he wishes to portray. In his restriction of the composition to a single figure, with a few accessories, and in his scrupulous dependence on the model, the novice stands revealed, even by comparison with his teachers. But this very reticence is a first and special testimony to his artistic genius, and the intensity of his endeavour. It is by its means, in fact, that the youth already surpasses his masters in thoroughness of method, in his treatment of light, and, above all, in his earnest effort to realise his subject.

A small, unimportant work, closely allied to the *Money-Changer*, both in its treatment and its genre-like motive, was formerly in the Orleans Gallery, where it was ascribed to Gerard Don, and has been lately discovered in the posession of Frau Mayer of Vienna. *A Savant writing by Candlelight* (Plate 4), represents an old man (Rembrandt's father) seated at a table. It shews an advance on the Berlin picture in the arrangement, the happier relation of the figure to the surroundings, the more skilful subordination of the details, and the more refined treatment of the light.

How quickly Rembrandt achieved freedom of artistic expression on these lines is shewn in a second study of the apostle Paul, in the Germanic Museum at Nuremberg, (*St. Paul seated at a writing-table*, Plate 3), almost identical with the earlier picture in arrangement. Here again the saint is represented meditating among his books, his figure set against a light wall, and brightly illuminated by the sunshine. But the accessories are fewer, less prominent, and more skilfully subordinated; the light no longer falls full on the head, but glances upon it with a piquant effect of illumination : there is a warmth and vigour in the sunshine, a breadth and decision in the treatment, which stamp the work as a little master-piece of its kind. And yet all internal evidences, the size, the arrangement, the model, the costume, alike point to the conclusion (the picture bears no date, unfortunately), that it was painted only about a year, or at most two years, later than the Stuttgart example.

Two pictures may also be assigned to the year 1628, as two have been assigned to the preceding year. The period to which we must refer *Samson captured by the Philistines* (Plate 6), in the German Emperor's collection (Royal Palace, Berlin) and *St. Peter among the Servants of the High Priest* (Plate 5), in Herr Karl von der Heydt's collection at Berlin, is fixed by the dates which follow the monograms on both pictures. The artist's progress is attested by his now attempting a composition of several figures. In the first work the problem is somewhat awkwardly handled, but in the second (a very small picture) it is solved with considerable skill and originality. In the *Samson*, the three principal figures are grouped in a curious manner, one behind and above the other; each figure betrays the pose of the model, and even this has not been very happily reproduced, as, for instance, in the attitude of Delilah. But there is originality and observation in the manner in which a Philistine gropes his way into the room, dazzled by the sudden light. In the *St. Peter among the Servants of the High Priest*, as many as nine figures are brought together in the narrow space. Some of these, such as the standing warrior in complete armour, are clumsy in form and attitude. But the illumination by means of a fire which appears to be outside the foreground of the picture, and by a candle, which lights up the persons in the background, the grouping of the figures round the fire, and the effect of the fire itself, surpasses anything hitherto accomplished, or even attempted, by Rembrandt's teachers. For this very reason, indeed, Rembrandt closely approaches that master who inspired Lastman and the whole group of contemporary Dutch painters in Rome, the German artist, Adam Elsheimer. We need only compare pictures by Elsheimer, such as Lord Elgin's " Deliverance of Peter from Prison ", at Broom Hall, and " Peter's Denial of Christ ", in the Accademia at Venice, with this work of Rembrandt's, to be convinced of this affinity.

The grouping of the figures in a high pyramidal form seems to have been a favourite arrangement of Rembrandt's for some time. This peculiarity, and various others they share with the *Samson*, enable us to assign several undated works by the master to the same period. First among these we may mention two compositions, the originals of which have disappeared, *The Baptism of the Eunuch* and *Lot and his Daughters*, both engraved by Rembrandt's pupil Van Vliet, and further preserved in a number of old copies. Copies of the former are especially numerous; the Oldenburg Gallery owns a replica, with slight variations, which closely approaches the master himself [1]. In the *Baptism of the Eunuch* the principal figures are piled one above the other as in the *Samson*. The accessories of landscape and costume are treated exactly as in the pictures described above; some are laboriously and minutely copied from nature, others put in hastily from memory, which 'as, for instance, in the drawing of the horses, often proves but an indifferent guide to the artist. This clumsiness in parts, together with the circumstance that the Deacon seems to have been painted from the same model as the *Saint Paul* in the Stuttgart Gallery, makes it very probable that the picture was, in fact, painted so early as 1628. The *Lot and his Daughters* is probably somewhat later, for here the arrangement is more natural, the situation more vividly realised, and the drawing happier than in the *Baptism of the Eunuch* and the *Samson*.

In these respects the *Lot*, as far as it is possible to judge from Van Vliet's engraving, and a poor copy of the last century in a private collection at Gotha, was

_____

1 These, and other missing pictures, will be reproduced in the last volume from copies or old engravings.

superior to a composition of the same period still extant in the original, *The Presentation of Christ in the Temple* (Plate 7), in the Weber Gallery at Hamburg. Here again the grouping takes the same pyramidal form. Three figures among the five, Joseph, the Virgin, and the Holy Child, are still awkward and perfunctory in drawing. But Simeon is a speaking, almost a familiar conception: he expresses to the Virgin his faith and happiness; the prophetess Anna, whose dark figure is sharply relieved against the somewhat crudely illuminated wall of the temple, has an almost fantastic dignity of bearing. Simeon is painted from the same model as the *Saint Paul* at Stuttgart, and the head of Anna is almost an exact reproduction of Rembrandt's first etchings of his mother, of the year 1628. Hence we have good grounds for assigning this date to the Weber picture.

I know of only one dated picture by Rembrandt painted in 1629. This is the *Old Man asleep by the Fireside* (Plate 8), in the Turin Gallery, ascribed in the Catalogue to Lievens, notwithstanding the perfectly genuine monogram. It seems to be a study of Rembrandt's father. I shall mention it again among the portraits of the latter.

Several other works by the young master which have been brought to light again within the last few years bear internal evidences of their execution at this early stage of his career. Madame Edouard André, of Paris, owns a *Christ with the Disciples at Emmaüs* (Plate 9), a rather larger picture than the Turin example, and greatly superior to the latter, but evidently of about the same date. The subject, which Rembrandt treated so often in later years, and with a depth and delicacy of emotion unapproached by any other artist, is handled with great originality, even in this youthful essay. Of course the simple, intimate and heart-stirring effect which characterises the pictures in the Louvre and at Copenhagen is entirely wanting here; the young painter seems to have aimed chiefly at a startling effect, both as to situation and light. His Christ is a magician, who strikes awe and superstitious terror into the disciples. The figure of the risen Saviour is still somewhat wooden in attitude, and its sombre mass stands out in violent contrast against the light wall. But the crouching apostle who worships in the foreground is rendered with great truth of expression, and set in the piquant broken light with a delicacy of pictorial effect that already proclaims a great master. The concealment of the light behind the principal figure, the harsh opposition of the dark masses to a crude concentrated radiance, the small subordinate light that serves to illumine the old woman in the background, are traits so closely akin to details in the *St. Peter among the Servants of the High Priest* that the André picture must obviously be bracketed with this as a work of 1628, or, at latest, 1629.

Pictorially, as regards illumination and treatment, this work marks the highest point of the young master's achievement during his Leyden period; but in composition and spiritual intensity it is surpassed by another picture in a private collection in Paris, the *Judas bringing back the thirty Pieces of Silver to the High Priest* (Plate 10), which was bought by Baron Schickler at the sale of the Martinet Collection. Here the young painter ventures upon a highly dramatic episode. The despairing traitor writhing at the feet of the High Priest, the contemptuous abhorrence of the latter as he turns aside, the compassion or horror depicted on the faces of the assembled priests and Pharisees, are rendered with a force, a psychologic subtlety, a dexterity of arrangement that justly called forth the admiration of contemporary connoisseurs in Holland. Of course, the novice's over-anxiety for startling effect, and his exaggerated characterisation, are no less apparent here than in the pictures already described. The laborious execution, the somewhat dry treatment of the colour in parts, and certain awkwardnesses of handling, betray the juvenile origin of the work, the types and costumes of which further shew it to be contemporary with the *Samson* and the *Presentation of Christ in the Temple*, and hence to belong to the year 1628, or, at latest, 1629.

This assumption is confirmed by the allusion to the picture in Constantin Huygens' lately discovered autobiography. Huygens, who recorded his impressions of Rembrandt's art while the young painter was still at work in Leyden, does not speak of the *Judas* as a very recent picture. The brilliant tribute paid to the artist by one of the most famous connoisseurs of the day, in his autobiography, is of the highest importance, throwing, as it does, an entirely new light upon his position among contemporary painters at this initial period, and Huygens' description and appreciation of the *Judas* is of scarcely less value to the critic of Rembrandt's youthful *œuvre*; for, so far as we know at present, it is the only extant reference by a contemporary to any of his juvenile pictures. Proofs that the works under discussion were really painted by the master are by no means lacking; the engravings made from them by contemporaries, the signatures on the majority of the works themselves (though these signatures vary, and differ from those of a later period, as is not un natural in the case of a young artist), their affinities one with another, and with Rembrandt's drawings and etchings of the same period, their relation to the art of his teachers and forerunners, notwithstanding their striking superiority to that art, and the germs we note in them of his later development — these are evidences which enable us to judge of the pictures with a confidence rarely warrantable in dealing with the first fruits of a great master's genius. But as a *pièce de conviction* for those who will only judge of Rembrandt, as of every other painter, by the acknowledged works of his maturity, and who therefore refuse to recognise the master in performances often crude, awkward and unattractive, this explicit statement by a contemporary such as Huygens is an important document.

The freer treatment and more correct drawing of the *David playing the Harp before Saul* in the Staedel Institute at Frankfort (Plate 16) make it probable that this was a work of, perhaps, a year or two years later. We mention it here, however, on the grounds of the close affinity in its costumes, its weird and pathetic sentiment, and its lack of definition in local colour, with the *Judas*. For the *Saul*, whose evil hour seems to be approaching, the artist appears to have used the same model as for his *Judas*.

Huygens' admiration for the *Judas* and for Rembrandt's youthful work generally — he recorded his high opinion of the artist as the greatest painter of the coming age when the latter was from twenty-three to twenty-four years old — is a surprising evidence that the judgment of contemporaries on these works differed widely from our own. This is further shewn by the numerous etchings and engravings after his early pictures, by Van Vliet, Savry and other engravers. The theatrical conception, the coarse and violent characterisation, the exaggerated expression and illumination, the fantastic costumes and accessories, suited the taste of the times, times in which the long and terrible schooling of the Dutch struggle for freedom had engendered feelings deep, indeed, but strong almost to coarseness. The same qualities appear in the works of Rembrandt's teachers and predecessors, and in those of several of his contemporaries, though not always in combination, and never so sharply and forcibly impressed upon their works. The manner in which Rembrandt harmonised these qualities, and gave intensity of dramatic force to his compositions by dazzling effects of light, aroused the universal respect and admiration of his countrymen.

All these early compositions are marked by a more or less scrupulous attention to the model, a testimony to the earnestness with which the artist entered upon every new task, depending solely on nature for guidance. It was by this means he was enabled, in a comparatively short time, to free himself from the conventional tradition of his teachers. But, on the other hand, his early pictures suffer to some extent from this very conscientiousness; they lack the freshness of invention, the finality so characteristic of Rembrandt's later works. The careful, almost painful exactitude of treatment, is extended to all the accessories. The artist studied costume from such Orientals and offshoots of Eastern races as he was familiar with in Leyden. The long, sleeveless gaberdine of the Dutch Jew, Turkish turbans and sashes, miscellaneous weapons, such as a Malayan creese, an Oriental leathern quiver with arrows, and a great two-handed sword, a steel gorget, a large water-bottle, and a few ponderous folios made up the sum of studio properties owned by the young Leyden master, and these he used with such insistence in certain compositions, that they give one the impression of still-life pieces in which figures have been introduced. Here again the young artist was probably influenced by older compatriots, inferior though they were to him in gifts. The still-life composition known as a " Vanitas ", an arrangement of various objects symbolic of mortality, which was peculiar to the sternly orthodox university town of Leyden, found its first exponent in the older Leyden artist, David Bailly, to whose works one of Rembrandt's first pictures, the *Money-Changer*, shews a marked affinity.

The treatment of light in Rembrandt's pictures, personal as it seems at first sight, was not an entirely new departure, due to the young artist alone. Several earlier painters of the Dutch colony in Rome, influenced partly by Caravaggio, partly by Elsheimer, had made the introduction of an energetic light, either sunlight or some artificial illuminant, the leading motive in their compositions. Rembrandt's juvenile method is closely akin to theirs; he has not yet adopted the uncertain, supernatural light of his maturer manner, but almost invariably chooses a decided, and very energetic sunlight or candlelight as the illuminating motive in his pictures. The variety with which he treats this motive, and the delicate observation he shews in the process, place the young painter far above his predecessors, although the violent oppositions, the crude lights, and black shadows of these early works proclaim them the productions of the novice.

In colour, Rembrandt's earliest pictures are of a very uniform character. The dominant tone is invariably a brownish hue, to which all local colours are subordinated. Light yellow or gleaming gold attracts the eye in immediate juxtaposition to neutral brownish or grayish tones in shadow; these, again, are blended with reds and blues, broken into violets and purples, with a fine instinct for colour harmonies and gradations.

The anxious care with which Rembrandt paints throughout from the model in these early compositions might naturally lead us to infer that his first essays were studies of heads, as was, in fact, the case with his etchings. But that no such initial process heralded his first pictures, shews, in the words of Huygens, that from the first the young master "strove, with conscious endeavour, after the highest".

The earliest dated study of a head extant, is a small autograph portrait in the Cassel Gallery, very slight in treatment, painted in 1629. Their analogies with this enable us to assign several similar heads to the same year; one or two among them may possibly belong to the year 1627; but these studies first become numerous and important in 1630.

It is an interesting fact in relation both to the art and character of Rembrandt, that he chose the models for such studies almost entirely from among the members of his own household. A large number of portraits and studies of heads by his hand, etchings as well as pictures, have been traditionally known from the earliest times as portraits of himself, his father, his mother, his wife, his son, his cook, etc. As, however, many of the supposed studies of these respective persons differ materially one from another, criticism was for a time very cautious in accepting any such designations. Some among them, indeed, were obviously flights of pure fancy; but many, on the other hand, have proved perfectly appropriate, in the light of that fuller knowledge of the painter's life given us by modern research. Recent discoveries have, in fact, enabled us to identify many persons of Rembrandt's *entourage* hitherto unknown, among these studies and portraits, in some cases on strong presumptive evidence, in others with absolute certainty. Even in his own times, for instance among the effects of his friend, the art-dealer Clement de Jonge (1679, various etchings figured as " Rembrandt's Moeder ", " Rembrandt's Fader ", " Titus conterfeyted ", " Rembrandt's concubin ", etc.

In the case of his youthful essays, it would not be unreasonable to argue that Rembrandt's choice of models from among his immediate surroundings was either a matter of chance, or one determined by a very justifiable economy. But we see that the practice was one he persevered in to the end of his days. When he was at the height of worldly prosperity, he produced a specially large number of such portraits, shewing that he satisfied an intimate desire by their execution, and painted his nearest and dearest over and over again, impelled by a sense of true family affection. Nor were these exercises without their purifying and ennobling effect upon his spiritual conceptions in general.

The earliest and also the most perfunctory of these studies of heads are autograph portraits. They are unimportant little pictures, sketchy in execution, dull in colour, black in the shadows — so unattractive, indeed, that it is only of late they have been accepted as genuine works. One is in the Cassel Gallery, the other in the Gallery at Gotha, a third in a private collection. It had never occurred to the young artist to make a dignified portrait of himself at the time when he painted these pictures. Like so many studies of himself among his etched work, contemporary with, or a little later than these, they are hasty impressions in which the painter made use of himself as the most readily accessible model from which to seize a pose, or an effect of light, or to solve some problem that interested him for the moment. It is from this point of view only that we must judge of these heads, and thus examined, they are of great interest as characterisations of the master. They cannot and must not be accepted as actual portraits; the young painter was never so ill-favoured and boorish in appearance as he sets himself down here; this is clearly shewn by the numerous portraits of himself painted soon afterwards. As finished pictures, they are scarcely more satisfactory, either in execution or illumination; the contrasts of light and shadow are invariably violent and exaggerated. But if we take them for what they unquestionably are, studies pure and simple, they are of great interest and value, as demonstrating the enormous advance made by the young Leydener beyond his compatriots. We see in these heads how he studied the varied emotions of the soul in his own features, how he rendered fear, astonishment, laughter, anger, how he subordinated colour to the strong effect of light in which he sought a novel medium for the expression of momentary feeling, a medium out of which he gradually evolved his " Rembrandtesque chiaroscuro ". This gives a peculiarly individual interest to what are in themselves an unimportant series of experiments.

The head in the Cassel Gallery, *Rembrandt with disordered hair* (Plate 11), is probably the earliest of these studies extant. It is almost boyish in expression, and if we assign it to the year 1628, we shall be placing it perhaps too late, rather than too early. The Gotha picture, *Rembrandt with an enquiring look* (Plate 13), as we have already noted, bears the date 1629; it was evidently a study for a figure watching some scene with anxious intensity, such as Rembrandt introduced, for instance, in *Samson*, and the *Baptism of the Eunuch*. A still smaller study, very simple and direct in conception, shews closer affinities with this Gotha head than any of the rest. The effect of light introduced is very energetic, but the execution as a whole is insignificant. Signor Meazza of Milan is the owner of this work *Rembrandt with a black Cap*. — Plate 14. The larger head of the *Rembrandt laughing, with a Cap* (Plate 15), in Count Nicholas Esterhazy's Collection at Nordkirchen, belongs to the same period. Of this M. Hengel of Paris owns almost an exact replica. In these pictures the shadows are clearer, the reflections more delicately observed. Here, as in the small head engraved by Van Vliet, recently acquired for the Hague Museum, the laughter is still forced, and has an effect of grimace.

An autograph portrait in the Hague Gallery, *Rembrandt with a steel Gorget* Plate 16, gives a much stronger impression of fidelity to the original than any of the above. The master has discovered the fine pictorial effect to be got by the juxtaposition of flesh tones, and those of polished steel. For the first time he introduces the small steel gorget which figures so repeatedly in later studies of heads, both his own and others. This portrait is no doubt the frankest and most faithful, and hence the most attractive rendering extant of the young Rembrandt, as he was in the year 1629, or early in 1630. In the Germanic Museum at Nuremberg there is a contemporary replica of this. It reproduces the original very faithfully, on a somewhat smaller scale, but is inferior in quality. Portions of the monogram and of the date 1630 are still visible, and it is not improbable that the copy, if not made by the master himself, was painted in his studio and that he signed it, after re-touching it.

The fine portrait of the youthful Rembrandt at the Hague is important on other grounds. It marks his abandonment of the small, almost insignificant scale he had hitherto adopted, a scale very unfavourable to breadth of conception. The portrait is almost life size. A bust portrait, on the same scale, unfortunately much damaged, is in Count Andrassy's Collection at Buda-Pesth (*Rembrandt in Morning Dress*. — Plate 17). It bears the date 1630, and is obviously almost contemporary with the Hague picture, to which it shews a close affinity in conception. It is coarser and hastier in execution, however, and not particularly attractive, either in illumination or treatment.

The largest and most important of the autograph portraits of this period is a life size, half-length figure, the hands omitted, at present in the possession of Messrs P. and D. Colnaghi, of London (*Rembrandt, young, with Cap and Feather*. — Plate 18). This picture, which is signed with a large monogram, and dated 1629, was included in the sale of the Buckingham Collection in 1848; it re-appeared in Christie's auction-room quite recently. It is painted with an evident anxiety to give a faithful, and at the same time a favourable presentment of the artist's own personality, and was probably either a commission, or a gift to some patron. The relations between Constantijn Huygens and the young Leyden master, as revealed to us by recent research, justify the surmise that this carefully executed portrait was painted for that distinguished patron.

The most significant feature of these portraits, especially of the last named, is the artist's gradual abandonment of the small scale to which he had hitherto confined himself, a change, which, as we shall see in the important pictures of this later time, materially affected the development of his style, producing modifications of considerable importance, and inciting him continually to renewed effort.

Rembrandt's etchings of this period shew that he experimented with his own portrait just as freely on the copper, practising himself in the new technique both by careful exercises, and hasty essays of infinite variety. The only drawing of this class known so far, is the very piquant example in the British Museum, probably a work of 1628 or 1629.

As we have already pointed out, these studies of the master's own head have but an occasional and qualified interest as portraits; the young painter sacrificed his own features ruthlessly to the exigencies of his experiment. It was far otherwise with the series of studies he made at the same time from an old couple, whom we are able to identify as his parents, the Leyden miller, Harmen van Rijn, and his wife. Not many years ago, nearly every portrait of an old woman by Rembrandt figured in collections as " Rembrandt's Mother ", especially if the sitter happened to be somewhat fantastically dressed. With the etchings, however, we are on firmer ground. The title has been bestowed from the first on a series of small studies of an old woman; in all these little heads or bust-portraits, with one or two exceptions, the same features are clearly recognisable. The hypothesis that Rembrandt's mother was the model for these is confirmed by various indications, slight yet significant. As long as the youthful Rembrandt remained an inmate of his parent's home, this sympathetic head is almost the only female study among his pictures and etchings; his pupils, Dou in particular, also painted it. After his removal to Amsterdam, the sitter disappears from his œuvre, save for a large portrait painted just before his mother's death. Rembrandt himself, and his pupil Dou as well, painted this old woman's portrait as pendant to the portrait of an old man, whom we may reasonably assume to have been Rembrandt's father.

Among Rembrandt's etchings, there are seven portraits in which we recognise his mother's features. The two plates of the year 1628, the earliest of his dated etchings, are of the number. One of these (Bartsch 355) is so happy, both as portrait and work of art, that it holds its own as a little masterpiece even when measured by the standard of Rembrandt's later work. None of the pictures are so early as this plate.

— 11

As far as they can be referred to the Leyden period, they seem all to have been painted about 1630-31; one, perhaps, as early as 1629.

A small study of an old woman's head, of which there are several replicas, all unsigned, and all of much the same quality, is closely akin to the early etchings, and to the autograph studies, both in its simplicity of conception, and in its suggestion of actual portraiture. One of these examples belongs to Dr A. Bredius *Rembrandt's Mother, small.* — Plate 19, and is exhibited at the Mauritshuis. The execution is careful, and even timid, the effect of light a very simple one, but the colour derives a peculiar richness from the tones of a gaily tinted shawl that peeps from under the drapery upon the head. Mr. W. C. Alexander of London owns a somewhat larger example, bluer in tone, and cooler in effect, in which the ornaments are more tastefully arranged. A third, of less importance, is in the Brunswick Gallery. It is possible that all these small pictures may be contemporary copies from some unknown original by Rembrandt himself. The head bears a striking likeness to a series of juvenile studies by Gerard Dou, representing Rembrandt's mother, more especially to the *Old Woman reading a Newspaper,* in the Dresden Gallery. This latter was indeed at one time attributed to Rembrandt; but when we compare it with the signed pictures by the master described above, we see, even in these early essays, how greatly Rembrandt excelled his pupil in conception and in knowledge of form, as in delicacy of chiaroscuro and richness of colour.

A work closely akin to the above, a portrait of the artist's mother, on a slightly larger scale, was in the Marquis of Exeter's collection till 1891. It was not sold by auction in that year, but, nevertheless, it no longer figures in the old collection. Here again the sitter wears the ample head-cloth, the folds of which fall upon a dark red mantle.

Very different to this small portrait is the larger and more freely treated study belonging to Mr. Arthur Sanderson of Edinburgh, *Rembrandt's Mother with a black Cap.* Plate 21. The broad and flowing fashion in which the artist indicates form, here by a full sweep of the brush, there by lines drawn with its butt-end in the moist paint, in a style peculiarly piquant and original, the cool flesh-tones against the rich blackness of the head-covering, the enamelled brilliancy of effect in the colour, the wonderful truth and insight with which the artist suggests an old age tempered by the freshness of a still vigorous mind, all these are qualities which give this study a place of the highest importance among the master's youthful works. The head of Anna the Prophetess in the *Presentation of Christ in the Temple* of the Weber Collection at Hamburg closely resembles this head in pose, adornment, and expression; but Mr. Sanderson's portrait is so greatly superior to the Hamburg picture technically, that it can hardly have been a study for this composition; it was probably painted some time after it.

The dimensions and arrangement of two other portraits of Rembrandt's mother (one apparently an unfinished study for the other) almost place them in the category of historical pictures, or character-studies. Both represent the old woman reading in a large Bible; she is richly dressed, and wears the ample head-covering of the ancient Dutch Jewesses. The one, *Rembrandt's Mother as Anna the Prophetess* (Plate 23), is in the Oldenburg Gallery and it is likely enough that the title bestowed on it expresses the master's intention. This picture is signed with the monogram, and dated 1631. The other, in Lord Pembroke's Collection at Wilton House, *Rembrandt's Mother, reading* (Plate 22), bears the very unusual signature "Rembrandt P." It is undated, but the comparatively unsuccessful drawing and arrangement incline me to place it before the Oldenburg picture; it may, indeed, have been painted so early as 1630. The manner in which the figure appears at a curiously low point of sight, half hidden by the large table with its monotonous green cover, and thrust away, so to speak, in the upper corner of the picture, the sharply foreshortened head, almost disappearing under the heavy folds of the deep violet head-cloth, betray the inexperience of the novice. In the drawing and treatment throughout, there are traces of haste and of a certain indifference. In the larger picture at Oldenburg these defects disappear. The old woman is seated in an armchair, in profile, almost her whole figure in evidence. Her fur-lined purple velvet mantle and head-dress of gold brocade, bound by a gaily tinted oriental scarf, make up a rich and harmonious chord of colour. Reflections from the warm sunlight that falls full on the open book in her lap touch the face, otherwise in shadow, and play upon the folds of the wide velvet mantle. Though the master has evidently dwelt *con amore* on the drawing and general treatment, the execution is free; the arrangement is finely pictorial in character, and in the touching effect produced by this dignified matronly figure, whose mind, already detached from earthly things, is absorbed in the study of her Bible, the work foreshadows the striking portraits of old ladies of the master's later period. This portrait was Gerard Dou's model for many of those early genre-pictures in which he treated the same motive.

A bust portrait, little less than life size, at Windsor Castle, *Rembrandt's Mother with a large Head-Covering* (Plate 24), a work very remarkable as regards colour and illumination, is more closely allied to Dr. Bredius' small early portrait in its simplicity of treatment and portrait-like effect, though the introduction of the full black velvet wimple lined with gold brocade, and the broad fur tippet give it a more fanciful appearance. The careful technique points to the year 1630, or the beginning of 1631, as the probable time of execution.

Among the numerous genre-like portraits of Rembrandt's mother by Gerard Dou, one in the Cassel Gallery has a companion-picture, the portrait of an old man. Dr. Eisenmann, the Director of the Gallery, when compiling his Catalogue in 1888, put forward the very pertinent suggestion that this old man might perhaps have been Rembrandt's father. Emile Michel took up the enquiry, and solved it in the affirmative, adducing ample proof in support of his contention. We may therefore accept the identity of the old man who figures in Dou's picture, and in a considerable number of Rembrandt's own studies and etchings, as unreservedly as we accept that of Rembrandt's mother in her reputed portraits. All these heads were painted while the young master was still working at Leyden; with the exception of two, which bear the date 1631, all the signed examples are dated 1630; several undated examples are probably earlier still, and we find the same model in compositions of 1627, such as the *Money-Changer*, and the *Old Man asleep* in the Turin Gallery. Like Dou, Rembrandt etched, and most probably also painted this old man's portrait as a pendant to his mother's; and Rembrandt's contemporaries and fellow-workers in Leyden, J. J. van Vliet and J. Lievens, etched several plates from the same model. The further fact, that Rembrandt etched and painted this head more often than any other at this stage of his career, but that it disappeared from his *œuvre* very shortly, clearly points to the miller, Harmen Gerritsz van Rijn, who died in April 1630, as the original. It may be objected that some of these portraits were not completed, in some cases not even begun, till after the death of the original. But this is, as a fact, an argument of little importance : one of the most interesting of Saskia's portraits bears the date of the year after her death.

Among Rembrandt's original etchings, there are six, which, in my opinion, represent his father. Besides these, we have a rendering by the hand of some pupil (Bartsch 293), and further, two out of the three well-known *Oriental Heads* of the year 1635, which Rembrandt, as his own signature attests, retouched only, and the authorship of which must be assigned to Lievens. The number of pictures for which Harmen was the model is still larger. These, like the etchings, are for the most part studies of heads. The list of such studies is perhaps scarcely to be looked upon as definitive, for it is only within the last few years that several unknown works of this particular class have been brought to light.

A small and delicately touched portrait of the miller, painted in warm brownish tones, and christened *Philo the Jew*, no doubt because of the fanciful dress of the model, who wears a turban-like cap with a gaily coloured scarf twisted round it, and a flowing fur cloak, bears the date 1630. This picture is in the Museum at Innspruck (Plate 26). In size, and in its daintiness of execution, it is closely akin to the little portrait of Rembrandt's mother in the possession of Mr. W. C. Alexander of London, which Michel declares to be the pendant of a similar small portrait in the Nantes Museum (Plate 26), a contention hardly borne out either by the size or arrangement of the latter. Another portrait of this group is the small picture belonging to Mr. Melville Wassermann of Paris (*Rembrandt's Father gazing fixedly at the Spectator*, Plate 25). Here he bears a double gold chain over his furred cloak, and a flat skull-cap on his bald head.

A second group of portraits consists of several busts, almost life-size, in which the artist's father is tricked out in fanciful martial array ; he wears a plumed cap, a burnished steel gorget, pearl earrings, and a gold chain. One of these pictures is in the Hermitage at Saint-Petersburg (*Rembrandt's Father in a plumed Cap*, Plate 27). It is octagonal in shape, and bears the artist's well-known monogram. It is cool in tone, and careful in execution. The same description will serve for the very similar portrait belonging to Mr. Chamberlin of Brighton (*Rembrandt's Father in a Cap with a blue Feather*, Plate 28), of which there is a good early copy in the Rijksmuseum of Amsterdam. A somewhat larger picture, remarkable for the dignified attitude and earnest expression of the sitter, passed from the Beresford-Hope Collection to that of Mr. W. H. Beers of New York (*Rembrandt's Father in a broad-brimmed Cap*, Plate 29).

Two studies of heads with dark caps, almost life-size, are simpler in treatment, and more obviously portraits of the original. One belongs to Dr. A. Bredius of the Hague (*Rembrandt's Father in a furred Cloak*, Plate 30), the other, formerly in the Habich Collection, is now in the Cassel Gallery (*Rembrandt's Father in indoor Dress*, Plate 31). Both, but more particularly the last named, are executed with the broad and sweeping touch characteristic of Mr. Sanderson's fine study of Rembrandt's mother. Another portrait, so much less free and confident in technique than these that I cannot ascribe it to the master himself, is the study with a turbanlike head-dress, in the Rotterdam Gallery, where it has hitherto been catalogued as by J. J. van Vliet.

In these portraits of Rembrandt's father and mother, and to some extent also in the autograph portraits, painted towards the close of the master's period of youthful development (the end of 1630 and the beginning of 1631), we recognise an earnest effort on the part of the young artist to free himself from the trammels of that minute and laborious manipulation acquired from his teachers, and described by Huygens as a characteristic of his style. As fresh confidence grew up with every new picture he painted, the master's instinct towards grand and striking effects gradually sought expression in larger dimensions and broader treatment. No doubt the influence of his contemporary and school fellow Jan Lievens, who worked in vigorous competition with him at Leyden, counted for something in this connection. In 1630, Huygens eulogised Lievens and contrasted his methods with those of Rembrandt, who, he tells us, strove after the achievement of great effects in small dimensions, whereas with Lievens « a sense of the grand and magnificent sometimes led to an exaggerated vastness of forms ». Huygens' testimony, indeed, makes it manifest that those very works of Lievens, hitherto supposed to have been executed under Rembrandt's influence. — studies of old men, of Orientals, of flaxen-haired Dutch maidens, were, as a fact, contemporary with Rembrandt's earliest essays, the productions of the years 1627 to 1630. The large *Soliman*, now in the Royal Palace at Berlin, is expressly mentioned by Huygens as already in the possession of the Stadtholder in 1630; and we can readily accept the early origin of this powerful, and in Huygens' opinion, "magnificent" picture, if we compare it with one of the best of Lievens' studies of old men, an example at Newbattle Abbey, dated 1629.

That the example of Rembrandt's friend and rival was not without its effect in stimulating him to a more imposing conception of form, is further demonstrated by a number of studies of this period, nearly all heads of old men, in which we cannot, as in the case of those above mentioned, identify the sitters. Some of these were long ascribed to Lievens, and there are some among them which the uninitiated still accept as his works. Closely akin as they are to similar heads by this artist, who occasionally painted from the same model as Rembrandt, they are easily distinguished from Lievens' work, even when unsigned, by their greater richness of colour, their more delicate chiaroscuro, and their more artistic and more intellectual treatment. Lievens is invariably drier in touch, more monotonous in colour and gaudier in his effects of light, in which a dull yellow tone predominates.

All these portraits of old men are life-size, or very nearly so. With rare exceptions, they bear no dates. One of such exceptions is the bust of an *Old Man wearing a large gold Cross on a long Chain*, in the Cassel Gallery (Plate 32). This very artistically treated work, remarkable for its piquant effect of light, is dated 1630. The head appears only once in the master's pictures and etchings, whereas that of another old man, with a broad brow, and thick beard, is of frequent occurrence. Two studies from this model, one rather larger than the other, are to be found respectively in the Schwerin Gallery and in Signor Fabbri's Collection at Florence (Plate 33). The larger example (that at Schwerin) is signed with the monogram. It is somewhat flat and light in tone, and soft in handling; the Florentine head is much more vigorous in illumination, and quite as animated in conception. A peculiarity in both, more strikingly apparent in the latter, is the treatment of the hair and beard, where the painter has sought to strengthen the effect by drawing the separate strands with the butt-end of the brush in the moist impasto. The Schwerin picture was formerly ascribed to Lievens, to whom various critics still assign it. The monogram differs from that used by Rembrandt at this period. The work may, indeed, be a study made by Lievens from the model who so often sat to Rembrandt.

This head in the Schwerin picture recurs again and again in the etchings (Bartsch 260, 291, 309, 315, 325 ; the dated examples belong to the years 1630 and 1631. Among Rembrandt's drawings, too, the same head appears more often than any other, and the examples are all dated 1630 or 1631. They are broad and vigorously executed studies in red chalk or charcoal, and are to be found in the Berlin Museum, the Teyler Institute, in Mr. Heseltine's Collection, and in the Louvre, which owns no less than three examples, in charcoal. The red chalk drawing in the Berlin Museum is a study for one of the two small pictures in the Louvre known as *The Philosophers*. These are both dated 1633; but this seems to me by no means a convincing proof that the drawing is of the same year. It is, indeed, so closely akin to others of 1631, that it probably belongs to that date. A little picture in the Stockholm Gallery, *St. Anastasius in his Cell*, bears such a strong resemblance to the Louvre *Philosophers* as to suggest that Rembrandt made the preliminary studies for these so early as 1631, though their actual execution was delayed till after his removal to Amsterdam, and the completion of the *Anatomy Lesson*. The same old man sat both for the *Philosophers* and the *Anastasius*. He reappears in an etching of 1639, for which Rembrandt perhaps made use of an old drawing in his portfolio. For the etching, *Joseph relating his Dreams*, of 1638 (Bartsch 37), a drawing of 1631 (sold at the Mitchell sale) was turned to account. The same model figures once more in the *Visitation* of 1640 at Grosvenor House. But this head occurs, too, in pictures of an earlier date than these drawings and etchings. We recognise it not only in the *Lot* and in the Philip of the *Baptism of the Eunuch*, pictures known to us only by Van Vliet's etchings, but further in the *St. Paul* of the Germanic Museum, and in Count Stroganoff's *Jeremiah*.

One picture in which this aged model figures remains to be noticed. It is another study of an apostle — the *St. Paul* so specially reverenced by the youthful artist — and is in the Imperial Gallery at Vienna (Plate 35). The Catalogue expresses a doubt as to its authenticity. The inscription it is said to have borne is no longer legible; the date, which used to be read 1636, was, probably, 1630. This we may infer, not only from the model, but from the whole composition, of which Rembrandt made both a drawing (in the Louvre, and a large etching (Bartsch 149 [1]), an exceptional circumstance in the record of his works. Both drawing and etching have all the characteristics peculiar to the year 1629-1630. In arrangement, too, the picture closely resembles the *St. Paul* of the Germanic Museum. If the composition, carefully and even anxiously considered as it is, strikes us as strangely uninteresting when compared with earlier works, if the handling seems hasty and wanting in tenderness, these defects are clearly due to the unaccustomed scale on which the young artist was working.

The intention of this *St. Paul*, of which there is a replica of much the same quality and size, but with some change of accessories, in Mr. M. C. D. Borden's Collection in New York (Plate 36), is made evident by another large figure of an Apostle, formerly in the Dudley Collection, and now in the possession of Mr. J. H. Harjes of Paris (*Saint Paul writing his Epistle to the Thessalonians*, Plate 34). Here again we have Saint Paul, as is indicated by the words from the second Epistle to the Thessalonians on the paper before him : Ερωτῶμεν δε ὑμᾶς. This picture has been

---

1. The drawing, a large one, in red chalk and charcoal, is obviously a study for the etching, which is of the same size, but reversed, for in the etching the Apostle holds the pen in his right hand, while in the drawing it is in his left. The etching is one of Rembrandt's first essays on a plate of large size.

hitherto assigned to the year 1636, on the strength of its affinity with the *St. Paul* in the Vienna Gallery; but evidences of early origin are even more pronounced in this than in the Vienna example, for here we have the model who figures only in Rembrandt's first pictures, the *St. Paul* of the Stuttgart Gallery, and the *Presentation in the Temple* of Herr Weber's Collection. This *Saint Paul* is more obviously a studio model than that of the Vienna picture; the colour is still greyer and cooler, the light still duller. The picture cannot be placed later than 1630; it should, indeed, perhaps be included among the essays of the year 1629. Both works are akin in conception and arrangement to those portraits of Rembrandt's mother at Oldenburg, Wilton House, etc., in which she figures as *Anna the Prophetess*, or some such personage. But in these feminine heads the young artist is more emotional in conception and more tender in execution.

On the strength of these preliminary essays, Rembrandt made his first attempt at a composition of several life-size figures in 1631 with *The Holy Family*, in the Munich Pinacothek (Plate 38) — an attempt in which he had more than a common measure of success. The subject he chose was one peculiarly suited to his powers : a rendering of quiet domestic happiness, glorified by a mysterious radiance, exalting the scene above those of ordinary daily life, from which it is nevertheless faithfully transcribed by a subtle observer of nature. Each separate figure is happily conceived and vividly portrayed; there is a fine sense of unity in the *ensemble*, and the accessories are skilfully subordinated. Comparing the picture with the master's later treatment of the same motive, we are, of course, sensible of a certain emptiness in the head of the Virgin, whose fond expression is perhaps a little exaggerated in its sweetness, of a somewhat disturbing insistence on the folds of the draperies, due to the young master's predilection for heavy, substantially lined materials, of a certain insipidity in the colours, and want of force in the illumination. A little picture in Mr. Boughton Knight's Collection (*The Holy Family resting during the Flight to Egypt*, Plate 37), may be looked upon as a sort of preparatory essay for the above. The gentle figure of the mother, her pretty features, and details such as the fur rug, are common to both pictures. The drawing and arrangement, the naïve crowding together of all the familiar antiquities of the young painter's studio, the coarse drawing of the tree-trunk and the foliage, and the colour generally, proclaim the affinity of this picture to those of the years 1629 and 1630. We shall therefore not be far wrong in assigning it to 1630.

The completion of the Munich picture coincides with Rembrandt's decision to quit Leyden for Amsterdam, which, as Orlers, his senior and fellow-citizen, tells us, his frequent visits had made him look upon almost as a second home. Here his pictures already ranked among the most coveted works of art of the period. The master's reputation, indeed, already rested upon achievements of such variety and originality, achievements on the diverse tendencies of which he had already laid the *impri-*

matur of distinctive artistic importance so unmistakably, that his determination to compete with his masters and other painters of note in the chief centre of Dutch activity was certainly not prompted by any exaggerated estimate of his own powers or successes. His fame in Amsterdam was due, not so much to his large, and somewhat coarse pictures and studies, as to a series of small and carefully finished compositions, the master-pieces of this initial period. To this series belongs the *Prophet Jeremiah* of 1630, in Count Stroganoff's Collection at Saint-Petersburg (Plate 39), a sorrowful old man, who has taken refuge in a cave with the treasures, among them a copy of the Scriptures, which he has saved from the destruction of Jerusalem. It would be difficult to speak too highly of this work, as far as it goes. It is distinguished by a refinement in the treatment of the chief figure, a masterly breadth in the handling of accessories and background, an accomplishment in the rendering of stuff and ornaments, a richness and harmony of colour, a warmth and brilliance of tone far beyond anything ever achieved by Gerard Dou in imitation of such works by his master. The old man, as I have already remarked, is the same model that figures in the *Lot*, and in various other pictures of this period.

A very similar picture of the following year, in which, however, the small figure is more subordinated to the wider space and its harmonious illumination, is in the Stockholm Gallery. This is the *St. Anastasius in his Cell* (Plate 40). Yet another study of an old man, alone, absorbed in mournful self-examination, belongs to the Prince de Rubempré of Brussels. It represents the penitent *Saint Peter in Prison* (Plate 41); the aged captive kneels on his straw pallet, his hands clasped in prayer. Striking as attitude and expression are in this work of the year 1631, the treatment of the space, and accessories recall the earlier *St. Paul* of the Stuttgart Gallery. The *Prophet Elisha*, in Mr. Lehmann's Collection, Paris (Plate 42), is peculiarly solemn in conception, artistic in treatment, and powerful in its effect of light. Robed in a white ephod embroidered with gold, a book in his hand, from which he looks upward with an inspired gaze, he advances towards a table, laden with various costly vessels dedicated to the service of the Temple. The freedom of handling which marks this work precludes the idea that it would have been painted before 1631 at the earliest: but its affinities of composition with the group of pictures now under discussion dispose me to class it among them.

All these works may be taken more or less as preparatory to the master's first composition of numerous figures, painted in 1631, the *Presentation of Christ in the Temple* (Plate 44), one of the acknowledged masterpieces of the Hague Gallery. Many studies and models, familiar to us in Rembrandt's early pictures, etchings and drawings, are to be recognised here in the group that gathers round the Holy Family, or among the devout multitude worshipping in the Temple. All these figures are brought together very skilfully and made to harmonise with the motive: and the wide and lofty space, the chiaroscuro of which gives such impressive solemnity to the composition, is managed with great delicacy of feeling, and lighted with the utmost dexterity. Architecture and figures bear the right relation one to the other; the latter lose nothing of their effect by the vastness of their surroundings. A comparison of the picture with the little etching of the year 1630, and the earlier version of the subject in the Weber Collection, will shew what progress the young artist had made in a few years.

Rembrandt attempted a kindred subject at this period, *The Raising of Lazarus* (Plate 45), in which he sought to win a like result, by different means. A little picture, unknown to connoisseurs till within the last year or two, and now in the possession of Mr. Charles T. Yerkes, of New York (formerly of Chicago), appears to be a very early and immature rendering of the theme, to judge by the hasty execution, the attitudes and expressions of the principal figures, the arrangement, and the curious grouping of the on-lookers, whose heads are piled one above the other. This picture can scarcely have been painted after 1630, and is probably a work of 1629. The master re-modelled the composition with great skill in the well-known large etching, in which he achieves a weird and striking, if not a deeply moving effect. That this etching was executed in 1633, as is generally supposed, seems to me improbable, taking into account its affinities with M. Yerkes' picture, and its still closer relation to a large red chalk drawing of the *Entombment* in the British Museum, dated 1630. The spacing and grouping of this drawing, even in respect to minor details, are so strikingly akin to those of the etching, that the two can hardly be divided by an interval of more than two years at the utmost. A comparison of the two is deeply interesting, not only as an illustration of the master's rich imagination, and skill in arrangement, but as an evidence of the increasing depth of emotion displayed in the treatment of each motive. The composition is so modified by comparatively slight alterations, that the difference of sentiment proper to the two themes is fully expressed.

Towards the close of his first period in Leyden, Rembrandt made his first essays in the rendering of the female nude. The two etchings, assigned with much probability to the year 1631, *Diana* (Bartsch 201) and the masterly little *Danae* (Bartsch 204), shew a great comprehension of the treatment of the nude. A little study for the *Diana*, recently discovered, is now in the possession of Mr. E. Warneck of Paris (See Plate 47). The young artist, who probably had no great choice of feminine models for the life, could scarcely have found one less attractive than this elderly sitter: but the enamelled treatment and the brilliant effect of the flesh tones shew great skill, even at this early period.

At about the same time Rembrandt began to make a reputation as a portrait-painter, a fact of much significance in connection with his removal to Amsterdam. Three portraits are extant with the date 1631, and there are further a few others, undated, which we may group with these on internal evidences. Comparing these with works so obviously of the nature of studies as the early autograph heads, and the pictures of the painter's father, his mother, and others, we may distinguish them as portraits proper. One among them, however, a *Young Man in a Turban and Oriental Shawl*, (Plate 49), closely resembles these studies as regards the fanciful costume of the sitter. It is a work in the Royal Collection at Windsor, which Emile Michel pronounced to be a portrait of the youthful Gerard Dou. To me, however, the type seems to differ considerably from that in Dou's portrait of himself, where the face is broader, and the nose shorter, while the eyes are very unlike those of the Windsor picture. An earlier work than this is the *Portrait of a Youth* (Plate 48) in the possession of Herr Adolph Thiem, of San Remo (formerly of Berlin). Its fat impasto in the carnations brings it into close relation with the female portrait belonging to Dr. Bredius, while its dark shadows recall those of the autograph studies painted about 1630. Another of Rembrandt's early male portraits, that of a man in the simple costume of a citizen of the day, is dated 1631, and bears the monogram $\mathcal{R}$, the characteristic signature of this initial period. It represents *A Savant seated at a Writing-table* (Plate 50), whom an ancient tradition of the Hermitage Museum, to which it belongs, describes as the writing-master, Coppenol. There is, however, no likeness at all between the features of this man and those of the famous calligraphist immortalised by Rembrandt's etchings, and the book and manuscript on the table before him indicate a voluminous, rather than a decorative writer. It is not unlikely that the original was some learned pundit of the Leyden University. The third and most important of these portraits (dated 1631) shews us Rembrandt already at work for an Amsterdam patron : this is the *Portrait of Nicolaes Ruts* (Plate 51), which passed, at the sale of the Adrian Hope Collection, into that of Mr. Joseph Ruston, of Lincoln. It represents a middle-aged man, in his winter costume, a fur-lined cloak and wide fur cap, standing by a chair, a letter in his left hand. The momentary quality of the conception, and the self-conscious attitude, emphasise the energetic cast of the features, the forcible expression of which is further enhanced by strong contrasts of light and shadow.

A couple of undated portraits on a smaller scale have so much in common with the above that they may be safely assigned to the period preceding Rembrandt's removal to Amsterdam. One, in the possession of Dr. Bredius at the Hague, represents *A Young Girl* (Plate 52). It is signed with the usual monogram, without the affix " van Rijn ", a form of signature which of itself lends considerable support to the ascription of the work to this early period. The exaggerated stress laid on certain individual peculiarities in the drawing of the head is a further evidence in the same sense: this very over-insistence gives a curiously fresh and naïve character to the work. The same incorruptible sincerity in the reproduction of nature makes itself felt in the handling, which is exceptionally tender and painter-like; the high and slightly purplish tones of the carnations foreshadow the treatment characteristic of the most " modern " tendencies of our times. Rembrandt painted a small full-length of this same young girl a little later : the *Young Woman standing in an Interior* (Plate 53), of the James Simon Collection at Berlin; the model has the same features, and appears to be of the same age as that of Dr. Bredius' picture. Here again the handling is hasty, especially in the hands. The problem which evidently absorbed the master's attention was the rendering of the highly pictorial effect produced by the figure in an interior brilliantly illuminated by sunshine, and full of varying reflections; this problem he solved with great skill, and with a breadth that gives a certain sketch-like quality to the study.

Rembrandt painted himself on much the same lines at this time. Of two little pictures which represent him standing in a room, the larger and more finished, in M. Dutuit's Collection at Rouen, bears the date 1631; in the other, owned by Madame Kums, of Antwerp (Plate 54), almost a replica of the former, he wears the same *quasi-Oriental* costume. It bears a false signature, and the date 1641. The fact that the painter is evidently of the same age here as in M. Dutuit's picture (about twenty-four years old) shews that it must have been excuted at the same early period. In both these pictures again, the task the artist has set himself is the rendering of a figure in the warm, sunlit atmosphere of a room full of the effects and reflections of light breaking in from outside. The choice of a small scale in these and similar pictures painted shortly afterwards, as also the rendering of the figure at full length, and in an interior, were certainly due, as we shall see later, to the influence of the Amsterdam portrait-painter, Thomas de Keyser. A genre-like study closely allied to the above, and painted probably 1631, is the *Young Savant at a Writing-table* (Plate 43) in the Brunswick Gallery.

THE REMOVAL TO AMSTERDAM

REMBRANDT was still an inmate of his father's house in the summer of 1631, as we learn from a document recently discovered in Dutch archives; but we find him domiciled at Amsterdam in 1632. His migration must therefore have taken place in the course of the winter, and it was probably more or less of a gradual process. It seems likely that the young Leyden painter found accommodation during his earlier sojourns in Amsterdam at the house of his friend, the art-dealer Hendrick van Uylenborch, who had a strong personal interest in attracting the artist to the city. Here he first began to think of settling at Amsterdam, and here inclination ripened into resolve, when Dr. Tulp (probably in January, 1632) offered him the important commission of a portrait-group of himself and his pupils. From Uylenborch's house Rembrandt, no doubt, chose his dwelling on the Bloemgracht, and superintended the installation of his modest bachelor plenishings, and his studio-gear. The cherished son, who had never left the paternal home save for short visits, no doubt would have wished his mother to arrange his little establishment in the great, strange city. But she was too old for such a task; and she appears to have sent her young daughter Lysbeth, the only unmarried member of the family, to provide for the young man's comfort, and keep house for him for a time. We have no documentary evidence to support this surmise, it is true; but as we have done already, and as we shall be able to do later, we may here turn to the master's works for information as to his life. The figure of a certain young girl appears so often among the portraits, and as a model for the pictures painted at the time of Rembrandt's removal, and during the first year of his residence in Amsterdam, that we must suppose her connection with him to have been a very close one. This is further evident from the fact that Rembrandt occasionally painted his own portrait as a pendant to hers, and that he represents her in the same fanciful style of costume as that in which he was fond of depicting himself, his father, and his mother at this period. As, further, there is a likeness between her and the painter, both in features and complexion, as her apparent age agrees with that of his sister Lysbeth, as she had already served Rembrandt as his model for several pictures painted at Leyden, and finally, as she disappears from his *œuvre* from the time of his betrothal to Saskia van Uylenborch, it is perhaps not over-bold to conclude that these pictures were all painted from Lysbeth Harmens, that this young sister arranged the master's home in Amsterdam, and kept his house there for the first two years of his sojourn.

We have therefore two landmarks, as it were, in the artist's work, by which his removal to Amsterdam is signalised; these are the *Anatomy-Lesson*, and the portraits of Lysbeth. Before tracing the course of his development and his activity in the capital, we will consider these works.

The *Anatomy-Lesson* (Plate 55), which Rembrandt was commissioned to paint by the famous anatomist, Nicolaes Pietersz Tulp, in January, 1632, and which he completed during the year, was acquired for the Gallery of the Mauritshuis from the Guild of Surgeons in 1828, by William I. King of Holland. It was long unquestioningly accepted as one of Rembrandt's greatest works, the masterpiece of his early period. This estimate of the picture is not so universal at the present time. The serious critic takes no exception to what may strike the general public as a repulsive motive; for the demonstration on the corpse itself has been so skilfully subordinated by means of the subdued light and the chiaroscuro, that the ghastly effect produced by such a theme in the hands of Rembrandt's predecessors, scarcely makes itself felt at all. What some eminent artists fall foul of in Rembrandt's famous work is a certain embarrassment in the drawing, and the unfortunate arrangement of the heads of the students. These strictures are not altogether groundless; on the other hand, little fault can be found with the conception as such. Here, as in the few portraits painted in 1631, Rembrandt is not primarily concerned with the individuality of his models; he conceives his group in the historic sense; he is intent on the rendering of an organic whole, a lecture, at which the attention of each member of the audience is strenuously concentrated on the propositions advanced by the speaker. The dramatic instinct so pronounced even in his earliest works, governs him so pre-eminently here, that it carries him beyond the mere transcription of portraiture, and impairs the sincere and perfect rendering of personalities. Rembrandt, indeed, gives less in this respect than many of his contemporaries and predecessors, while on the other hand he far surpasses all these masters in the unity of his conception. If, even so, he falls something short of complete success here, or overshoots the mark to some extent there, so that the effect produced is not altogether satisfactory, we recognise however in his effort the germ of the great innovation he was destined to work out in portraiture : the representation of the inner man of his model, speaking directly to the heart of the spectator. Even in this early work, he achieves one complete success in this direction, and that in the rendering of the chief personage, Dr. Tulp himself. This is a pleasing, a life-like, a most significant conception. In the expression of the face, in the action of the hands, as he demonstrates to his pupils, there is such simplicity and distinction, something so eloquent and convincing, that no other Dutchman, before or after Rembrandt, could have painted such a figure. Rembrandt himself produced few portraits to surpass that of Tulp in these qualities.

With regard to the second of what we have called the landmarks of his first years at Amsterdam, the figure of the youthful female model who appears so repeatedly in portraits and pictures painted immediately after the removal, we may say that the hypothesis of her identity with Rembrandt's sister is almost universally accepted on the evidences we have described above. The portraits in question are now commonly spoken of as portraits of Lysbeth Harmens. Émile Michel accepts this view, with the qualification that he takes one or two of the portraits, I include among those of Rembrandt's sister, to be rather studies of the master's betrothed, Saskia van Uylenborch.

The appearance of a second youthful female figure in the artist's studio immediately after, and in some instances at the same time with the first, certainly makes it difficult to discriminate very exactly between the portraits of the two, especially as these young girls were much of the same age, that both had fair hair and complexions, and that their features were very similar in type. This general likeness is further strengthened by Rembrandt's practice of treating the portraits of persons closely connected with himself rather as studies than as faithful likenesses, and making the actual reproduction of their features a secondary consideration. At this time, too, the young master was still hampered in his rendering of individual traits by that generalisation of forms he had acquired from his teachers. It is easy to see how this tendency would have influenced him when he first painted Saskia, and how, involuntarily, he gave the more familiar cast of his sister's features to those of the other young girl. Some light will, I hope, be thrown on this question by the grouping together in this volume of all the portraits I have classed as those of Rembrandt's sister. This group will be followed later by one of all the earlier portraits of Saskia. In both groups several pictures hitherto unknown or overlooked will be included.

The characteristic differences in the two feminine types seem to me the following. In spite of the likeness between the two, Saskia was distinctly prettier than her sister-in-law. The latter's features closely resemble her brother's; she has a short, somewhat thick-set figure, inclining to *embonpoint*, an oval head, a small nose, thickening at the tip, a small, somewhat compressed, and rather ugly mouth, a high, arched forehead, small, lively, pale-blue eyes, a long ear with a remarkably small lobe, and thin, reddish, frizzled hair. Saskia, on the other hand, though apparently small of stature, too, is slenderer and more regular of feature than Lysbeth. The shape of her head is more refined, her nose is longer and more delicate, her eyes more almond-shaped, brown in colour, and kindly in expression; the eye-brows are full and arched; the forehead is not particularly high, the ear regular in shape, with a large lobe, the hair of a reddish brown, and, in the later portraits, of a chestnut colour, more luxuriant in growth, and less frizzled than Lysbeth's.

Of course it is not possible to describe features with photographic accuracy from studies such as these, especially as Rembrandt allowed himself a certain degree of licence in each, subordinating or emphasising particular traits to suit the requirements of the effect of light, the expression, etc., the special problem, in short, he had set himself to solve. These pictures, as we have already pointed out, were, as a rule, studies, with the object of rendering the impression of the *ensemble*, rather than actual portraits.

In order to subject the studies of these two women to a more exhaustive scrutiny, experts have very properly compared them with the compositions in which the originals served as models to the artist. After such comparison, Michel came to the conclusion that Saskia figures in a series of pictures, painted for the most part in 1632, in which I had pronounced for the identification of the model with Lysbeth, an opinion I still venture to maintain. Various extraneous evidences seem to me to strongly support my theory. Even if it were probable that Saskia was in Amsterdam as early as 1632, and that Rembrandt had already made her acquaintance, it is impossible to suppose that the adopted child of a strict Protestant clergyman would have been allowed to sit to the young artist for his compositions, and become to some extent his regular model. Michel, however, is of opinion that Saskia was Rembrandt's model for the *Minerva* in the Berlin Museum, for the *Rape of Proserpine*, the *Rape of Europa*, and for the *Jewish Bride* in the Liechtenstein Gallery, all of which were painted about 1632, and were works demanding long and frequent sittings. This would scarcely be looked upon as decorous, even in the present day, and in the rigid Calvinistic Holland of that period, more especially for the inmate of a clergyman's household, such a possibility seems to me totally inadmissible. In addition to this, we have the fact that the person who sat for these pictures had certainly served the painter as model in his Leyden days. This will hardly be disputed after an examination of the Virgin in the *Presentation in the Temple*, of 1631, in the Hague Museum, and of one of the female figures in the *Lot and his Daughters*, of 1630, preserved to us in Van Vliet's engraving. In these two instances there can be no question of Saskia, for at the time they were painted Rembrandt had never seen her. On the other hand, a comparison of these figures with the acknowledged portraits of Lysbeth seems to me so convincing as to the similarity of type, that I cannot but accept Rembrandt's sister as the model for the female figures in all these pictures. Involuntarily, indeed, the painter's brush seems to have evoked some reminiscence of her type in later works, such as the various versions of the *Flora* (the so-called *Jewish Bride*), and the *Sophonisba* at Madrid, though, consciously or unconsciously, certain features of his youthful betrothed or wife seem to have crept into the conception.

All the portraits in which I recognise Lysbeth Harmens without any sort of hesitation are dated, with the exception of such as are merely replicas; five among them belong to the year 1632, and two to 1633; they are all busts, for the most part oval in shape, and, with one exception only, they do not shew the hands. A very characteristic example, and one it would be difficult to confuse with portraits of Saskia, is the oval bust in the Brera at Milan (Plate 56) in which the small features are very carefully rendered; the effect of light and colour here is a peculiarly powerful one, and the adornment of the sitter with a black veil and purple gown with a rich gold border produces a harmony of great splendour.

This picture is very closely akin to the portrait which passed from the Secrétan Collection to the Liechtenstein Gallery (Plate 57). In this the young girl is painted nearly full-face, without any covering on her head, in a reddish mantle with a wide border of gold embroidery. The artist has achieved a fine pictorial effect in the rendering of the fair light red hair illumined by strong sunshine; the expression of the face is pleasant and almost child-like; the features unusually delicate.

The simpler bust-portrait of *Rembrandt's Sister* (Plate 65), in the possession of Baroness Hirsch, in Paris, is marked by the same child-like, winning expression, although, according to the inscription it bears, this was not painted till 1633. Here the sunlight falls almost full upon the head, whereas in a very similar portrait belonging to the Marquise de Carcano, of Paris (Plate 62), the light glances off the head to the left, leaving one side of the face in rather too deep a shadow. Another picture of this class has lately passed into the Gallery of Herr Alfred Thieme, of Leipzig, from an English Collection (Plate 59). It is obviously an unfinished work; the hair is only laid in with an under-paint, and consequently appears quite dark; the shadows are unrelieved by any reflexions; and in various other details we miss the finishing touches.

Another, differing in some essentials from the above, more finished, cooler in tone, and more complex in gradations, is a very fine bust portrait in Sir Francis Cook's Collection at Richmond (Plate 58), in which the sitter wears a toque with a green feather.

Lord Leconfield's oval bust portrait at Petworth (Plate 60), where the face is seen rather more in profile, is particularly important in connection with the question of identity. It is the pendant to a *Portrait of Rembrandt* by himself (Plate 61), in the same Collection, painted in the year 1632. Now the painter, as we know from an inscription by his own hand, was not betrothed to Saskia van Uylenborch till June, 1633. It will not be contended, therefore, that this could be a portrait of Saskia;

and yet this particular picture bears a strong resemblance to several of the earliest portraits of Saskia. One of the series described above (that in Baroness Hirsch's Collection) was also sold by auction in Paris some twenty years ago as a companion-piece to an autograph portrait of Rembrandt.

Two profile portraits of the year 1632 are put forward by Émile Michel as portraits of Saskia; one is in the Stockholm Museum, the other in Madame Édouard André's Collection, in Paris. In the Stockholm picture (Plate 63), however, we find a reproduction in profile of the same thick-set figure, the same round and bossy head, and the same compressed mouth that characterise the full-face portraits of Lysbeth we have just been considering. It seems to me therefore beyond question that the same model sat for both. There is more room for doubt as regards the André picture, formerly in the Haro Collection. The young girl here represented in profile certainly bears a strong likeness to the famous and fully authenticated profile portrait of Saskia with a broad-brimmed plumed hat in the Cassel Gallery. The more slender type, the more distinguished bearing, the longer and straighter nose, taken in conjunction with the simple costume of the day, unadorned by any such fanciful accessories as we are accustomed to find in portraits of Rembrandt's relatives, incline me to look upon this as a first portrait of Saskia van Uylenborch, among whose authenticated portraits we shall therefore include it later on.

There are two exact replicas of the Stockholm picture, both undated. One (Plate 64), until lately in Lord Denbigh's possession at Newnham Paddock, and now in Mr. Alexander's Collection in London, is quite equal to the Stockholm picture, and appears to me unquestionably by the master's own hand. The other, a somewhat smaller version (without the hand and fan), belonging to Mrs. Seymour, of London, would no doubt be accepted as a work of Rembrandt's if it stood alone ; but taking it in conjunction with the two larger and finer works, we can hardly suppose it to be more than a replica, executed under the master's direction by some gifted scholar.

All these portraits of Lysbeth Harmens belong to the year 1632, with the exception of Baroness Hirsch's example, which is dated 1633. Another portrait of this latter year (Plate 66), larger, and differing in some respects from the above, came to light not long ago in Mr. Massey Mainwaring's Collection, from which it passed to Mr A. Polowtsoff of St. Petersburg. In this the identity of the model is more questionable. It is simpler than most of the others in costume, and in the treatment of the light and the personality of the young girl is more carefully rendered; the somewhat rigid cast of the features common to many of the earlier portraits, is no longer noticeable; the head is more fully developed, and more life-like. If we compare it with the perhaps unduly childish and naive head of the Baroness Hirsch's picture, of the same year, it seems scarcely credible that the same young girl was Rembrandt's model in both. The large, round, somewhat prominent eyes, the full lips, the almost exuberant contours at least threw considerable doubt on the subject. There is, of course, a certain general likeness, especially in the shape of the head, the hair, the complexion and the figure; the sitter, too, wears the same costume in each, though it is differently adjusted, and the young girl of the Polowtsoff example is more richly adorned with ornaments than the other. It seems probable that the original was closely connected with Rembrandt in some way, even if she is not to be identified with Lysbeth Harmens.

As I have already said, we find the master making use of these studies of Lysbeth's head for various compositions of the same period, all of the year 1632, as those which are dated proclaim, and as we may safely conclude from the character of those which are undated. A couple of these are scarcely more than elaborate studies, while two others are richer compositions, of considerable interest in their bearing on the master's development.

The *Toilet of the Jewish Bride* Plate 69 in Prince Liechtenstein's Collection at Vienna, belongs to the former category. In dimensions, as in execution, finish, and artistic effect, it is one of the most notable works of the year 1632. The young maiden, in whom we recognise Rembrandt's sister, Lysbeth, is seated before us, receiving the finishing touches of her magnificent toilet; an old woman behind her, whose features are those of Rembrandt's mother, combs out her waving, golden-red hair, which is confined in front by a jewelled clasp with a small feather. The deep purple mantle with the broad gold trimming, and the white pleated chemisette drawn up to the throat are the same as those worn by Lysbeth in the Brera and Stockholm portraits, the former of which, indeed, might almost be a study for this picture.

The title of *Jewish Bride* is common to this work, to a series of single female figures gaily adorned with flowers, and to a few well-known etchings, all of somewhat later date. We can shew the designation to be a misleading one as applied to the later pictures, by reference to the title by which they were known in Rembrandt's own time. And even in the case of this early work, I am inclined to doubt that Rembrandt had any Jewish bride in his mind at all, whether from the point of view of an essay in genre, or, what is perhaps more akin to his conception, that of a familiar rendering of some heroine of the old Testament. It was just at this time that Rembrandt began to busy himself with subjects from mythology and Roman history. Nearly all the female figures he painted or etched at this period illustrate themes of this nature. Is it not more likely, therefore, that we have here his conception of some beauty famous in Roman story, such, for instance, as Cleopatra?

A smaller picture, or study. the original effect of which is a good deal discounted by early injuries either by fire or the heat of the sun, is in the Berlin Gallery (Plate 68. It represents Lysbeth almost in the same costume, seated at a table, her long light-red hair unbound. A crown of laurel leaves, in which one spray of blossom is entwined, holds her hair together; on the table lie books and musical instruments; weapons hang against the wall, among them a shield with the Gorgon's head. It seems probable, therefore, that the master meant to depict a Minerva. A similar female figure, in which the attributes again suggest a Minerva, is in the possession of M. Pol-Charbonneaux, of Reims (Plate 67).

It seems probable for two reasons that these heroic figures were derived from mythological rather than Biblical sources, firstly, the existence of the contemporary etchings of *Danaë* and *Juno*, and secondly, that of two larger compositions, in which Lysbeth again figures. These are the two remarkable pictures which, until quite recently, were either looked upon with grave suspicion, or rejected by critics of Rembrandt's works. And yet they are peculiarly characteristic of his early period, and have no affinity with the works of any other master. They represent *The Rape of Proserpine* and *The Rape of Europa*, but are not pendants, as might be supposed. The *Rape of Proserpine* Plate 70, which probably came into the Royal Collection at Berlin as part of the Orange inheritance, is an upright, oblong panel; it was originally known as a Rembrandt, but entered the Berlin Museum as a work of Van Vliet, just as the *Minerva* mentioned above figured in the old Catalogues as the work of Ferdinand Bol. The authenticity of the *Rape of Europa* Plate 71 was openly challenged at the Morny sale in 1865, in spite of its signature *RL van Ryn 1632*. The purchaser's name was kept a secret. It was not until lately that the picture came to light again in the possession of the Princesse de Broglie, *née* Say, Paris. The two pictures have much in common, but the *Rape of Europa* is decidedly superior to the other, not only in condition, but in respect of the composition, and the beauty of the distant landscape. There is a touch of something coarse and boorish in both, more especially in the *Proserpine*, though this is redeemed to some extent by the passion and vigour of the conception. These compositions of Rembrandt's impress us as illustrations of the antique myths of scholastic literature, translated into the popular language of Dutch folk-lore. The artist approached his subject in all seriousness, and with the best intentions as regards archæologic truth, and it was this manner of treating his theme which ensured the warmest approval from his contemporaries. This is evident from the comparatively large number of such mythological subjects painted in this, and in the following year. By his rendering of the brutal violence of Pluto to the innocent princess as she gathered flowers in the fields of Enna, Rembrandt seeks to realise all the gruesome terror of a tale of magic. Proserpine, helpless in the arms of the god, tears his face with her nails, and her maidens cling so desperately to the long silken robe of their mistress that they are dragged along in the wake of the fantastic gilded chariot, with which the fiery black horses will presently disappear into the abyss. In the *Rape of Europa*, the princess' attendants first become aware of the stratagem practised by the god in the form of the bull, when they see him dashing into the stream with the young beauty on his back. The frantic despair of the *Proserpine* is therefore appropriately replaced here by a strained and anxious attention; the landscape, too, with its delicate twilight tones, is so much more important in the *Europa*, that the effect made by the individual figures is less forcible. The dense clump of trees, the thistles and lettuces of the foreground, the team of horses, the *baroque* chariot and its negro-driver, are those theatrical « properties » derived from Rembrandt's master, Lastman, which we find in the *Baptism of the Eunuch*, the *Rape of Proserpine*, and other early compositions. On the other hand, the ancient town, and the stone bridge leading to the haven, with its picturesque old crane, shew both keen realistic observation, and grandeur of invention and temperament. This landscape, indeed, foreshadows those produced by the master towards 1639.

The most casual examination of these pictures will convince the student of the striking similarity between the female figures, in their costumes, their forms, and more or less even in their features, with those female figures I have identified with Lysbeth Harmens. In the *Rape of Europa*, the princess herself resembles Lysbeth, and one of her play-fellows on the bank has exactly the profile of the Stockholm portrait. In the *Rape of Proserpine*, she again serves as model for the principal figure; and the features and contours of the attendant maidens also shew how the master was haunted by her type as he painted them.

CATALOGUE

OF

REMBRANDT'S PICTURES

PART I.

1

THE MONEY-CHANGER

THE MONEY-CHANGER

An old man with a short beard, wearing a cap, is seated behind a table, testing a coin by the light of a candle he holds in his left hand. His features are those of Rembrandt's father. Ledgers and parchments are piled on the table, which is covered with a dull green cloth; beside them a pouch, a scale for weighing gold, and a few coins. A cupboard stands open near a stove in the background to the left.

Small half-length figure.
Signed on a book to the left : *R. 1627*.

Oak panel. H. 0ᵐ,32; w. 0ᵐ,42(¹).

Bode, p. 367, n° 33; Dutuit, p. 25, n° 354; Wurzbach, n° 28; Michel, pp. 26, 551.
Bredius, Nederl. Kunsthode, 1881, p. 182.

Van Eversdijck Collection. The Hague, 1766 (Terwesten, p. 533).
Sir Francis Cook's collection, Richmond.
Sir Charles Robinson's collection, London. Presented by him to the Berlin Museum, in 1881.
Berlin Museum.   (N°. 828 D in the Catalogue.)

(¹) The metric system of measurement is retained throughout this catalogue.

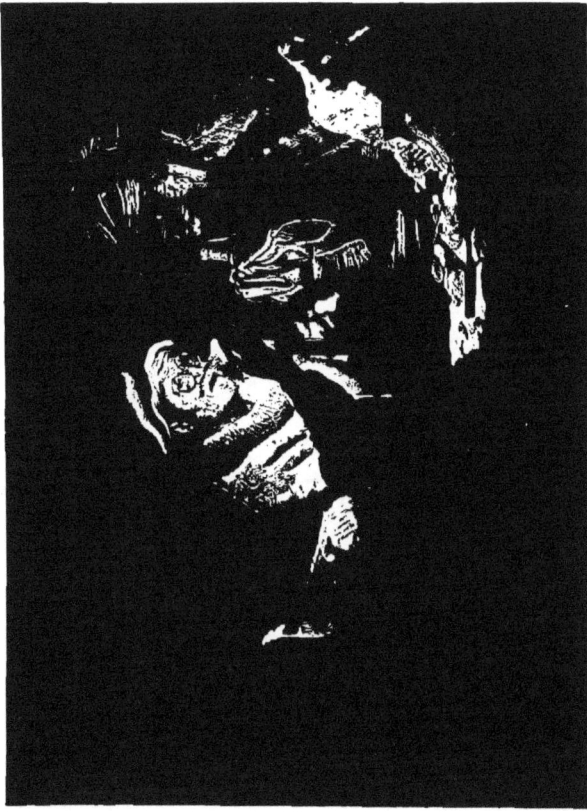

ST. PAUL IN PRISON

(ROYAL MUSEUM, STUTTGART)

ST. PAUL IN PRISON

(ROYAL MUSEUM, STUTTGART)

The Saint, seated on a bench against a brilliantly illuminated wall, rests his chin meditatively on his right hand, and holds a book on his lap with the left. He is bare-headed, and has a long white beard. He wears a steel-gray sleeveless over-dress, shewing the grayish-purple, green-lined sleeves of his tunic, and sits upon a reddish green drapery. Beside him, to the left, books in brown bindings, a wallet, and a large two-edged sword. Above, to the left, a portion of a grated window, from which the light falls on the figure.

Small figure, full length.

Signed on a paper lying on the Apostle's lap : *Rembrand fecit*, and a little lower down, on the bench : *R. f. 1627*.

Oak panel. H. o⁻,70; w. o⁻,58.

Etched by O. Baldinger, for the *Zeitschrift für bildende Kunst*, 1874, with a descriptive notice by A. Woltmann.

Vosmaer, p. 84, 486: Bode, p. 367, n° 122; Dutuit, p. 31, n° 98; Wurzbach, n° 116; Michel, pp. 26, 554.

Schoenborn-Pommersfelden Collection, sold in Paris, 1867.
Royal Museum, Stuttgart. (N° in Catalogue, 328.

ST. PAUL, BY CANDLELIGHT

(GERMANIC MUSEUM, NUREMBERG)

ST. PAUL, BY CANDLELIGHT

(GERMANIC MUSEUM, NUREMBERG)

Seated, facing the spectator, in front of a brightly illuminated wall. His right arm hangs, pen in hand, over the back of his chair. His left hand rests, palm uppermost, on the table. The Apostle gazes meditatively before him; he has gray hair, and a thick beard. His dress is a dull, grayish-yellow, sleeveless robe, girded with a parti-coloured scarf, over a tunic of thick gray material. A table stands by him to the right, covered with a dark greenish brown cloth, on which lie several folios. Behind these, a candle. Three yataghans with variegated tassels hang against a wooden pillar.

Small figure, nearly full-length
Painted about 1628.

Oak panel. H. 0m,47; w. 0m,39.

Exhibited at Berlin in 1890, n° in Catalogue. 222.

Bode, pp. 366, 636; Dutuit, p. 41, n° 103; Wurzbach, n° 36; Michel, p. 554.
Mittheilungen aus dem germanischen Nationalmuseum, 1891, p. 3.

Baron von Fechenbach's collection, sold at Berlin in 1882.
Bodeck-Ellgau Collection, Heidenfeld, near Schweinfurt, sold at Cologne, 1890.
Germanic Museum, Nuremberg. N° in Catalogue, 306.

A SAVANT STUDYING BY CANDLELICHT

(MADAME MAYER'S COLLECTION, VIENNA)

A SAVANT STUDYING BY CANDLELIGHT

(MADAME MAYER'S COLLECTION, VIENNA)

An old man seated to the left at a table, writing. His gray head is crowned by a high, dark biretta, with a narrow brim; over his tunic he wears a dark gray mantle of some heavy material. A large folio, the dark bulk of which stands out sharply against the light, conceals a candle, which illuminates the wall, and two or three objects on the right, among them a globe. A letter is fastened to the wall.

Small, half-length figure.
Painted about 1627, and closely akin to the *Money-changer* in the Berlin Gallery.

Copper. H. 0m.135; w. 0m.135

Etched as the work of Rembrandt by J.-B.-P. Lebrun. Later erroneously ascribed to Gerard Dou on the strength of the obviously modern signature G. D. F., to the letter on the wall.

Lebrun Collection, Paris, close of the eighteenth century.
Collection of Citoyen Robert, *ci-devant* Saint-Victor, at Rouen.
Dubois Collection, Vienna.
Herr Fr. X. Mayer's collection, Vienna.
Madame Mayer's collection, Vienna.

ST. PETER AMONG THE SERVANTS
OF THE HIGH PRIEST

(HERR KARL VON DER HEYDT'S COLLECTION, BERLIN)

ST. PETER AMONG THE SERVANTS
OF THE HIGH PRIEST

(HERR KARL VON DER HEYDT'S COLLECTION, BERLIN)

Peter in a crouching attitude to the left, his figure illuminated by the glare of an invisible fire; in front of him, a little to the right, a seated warrior, his back to the spectator; behind him another, asleep, leaning over his shield. Two soldiers stand behind Peter, talking together, the one to the right in complete armour. In the background to the left, four armed men in a group round a taper.

Small whole-length figures.
Signed in the lower right-hand corner ✒ *1628.*

Copper. H. 0ᵐ,22; w. 0ᵐ,17.

Etched by W. Rohr for *Die Graphischen Künste*, 1881.

Exhibited at Berlin in 1883.

Bode, p. 373, n° 45; Dutuit, p. 41, n° 95; Wurzbach, n° 37; Michel, pp. 30, 553.
Bredius, Nederl. Kunstbode, 1881, p. 182.

In the possession of the picture-dealer Sagert, Berlin, 1881.
Otto Pein Collection, Berlin; sold at Cologne in 1888.
Herr Karl von der Heydts' collection, Berlin.

SAMSON CAPTURED BY THE PHILISTINES

(ROYAL PALACE, BERLIN)

SAMSON CAPTURED BY THE PHILISTINES

(ROYAL PALACE, BERLIN)

Samson lies on the ground asleep, his head in the lap of Delilah, who is seated on a step. He wears a tunic of sulphur-yellow, girded with a gaily coloured striped scarf, from which hangs a yataghan. Delilah, dressed in a violet robe, bordered with a wide embroidery of blue flowers on a gold ground, holds the shorn locks in her right hand, and turns towards the Philistines, who are stealing into the room. One of these, a bareheaded, bearded man, in a short yellowish brown tunic, with a dark plaid folded squarely across it, holds a sword behind him in his outstretched right hand, and is about to seize Samson with his left. Another, a helmet on his head, and a drawn sword in his hand, looks in through a door to the right, behind the brown bed-curtain. In the foreground a plate, and two or three flagons of various metals.

Small full-length figures.
Signed on the step to the left with the monogram ℛ 1628.

Oak panel. H. 0ᵐ,60; w. 0ᵐ,49.

Exhibited at Berlin, 1890, n° in Catalogue, 221.

Bode, p. 370, n° 91; Dutuit, p. 26, n° 22; Wurzbach, n° 32; Michel, pp. 27, 551.
Bredius, Nederl. Kunstbode, 1881, p. 182.

Probably included in the Orange bequest, 1676.
The property of His Majesty the German Emperor, Berlin.

THE PRESENTATION OF CHRIST
IN THE TEMPLE

(HERR ED. F. WEBER'S COLLECTION, HAMBURG)

THE PRESENTATION OF CHRIST IN THE TEMPLE

(HERR ED. F. WEBER'S COLLECTION, HAMBURG)

The aged Simeon kneels near a pillar to the right, in the Temple, his face in profile. On his left arm he supports the radiant, half-naked body of the Infant Saviour; his right hand is outstretched in exhortation to the Virgin, who kneels with clasped hands, gazing anxiously at the Child. The High Priest wears a light, violet gray robe, with a collar of fox-skin; Mary has a blue mantle drawn over her head. Joseph kneels a little further to the left, his back almost turned to the spectator. He holds his hat in his clasped hands, and wears a dark brown dress.

Behind the group stands Anna the Prophetess, in a gray gown, and a head-dress of many coloured striped material; she raises both hands in benediction. Her dark figure stands out in strong relief against the sunlit wall. To the right a candelabrum, and a flight of steps.

Small figures, full-length.
Signed in the right hand lower corner : *Rembrandt f.*
Painted about 1628.

Oak panel. H. 0m,555; w. 0m,435.

Etched (reversed) by Weisbrod and Lebas for the " Lebrun Gallery ", in 1792; by W. Unger for the " Weber Collection", n° 1, 1891.

A (fancy?) drawing by Stolker in the British Museum, representing Rembrandt's studio, shews this picture on the easel.

Smith, n° 66 and 67; Vosmaer, p. 489; Bode, p. 368, n° 97; Dutuit, p. 41, n° 51; Wurzbach, n° 92; Michel, pp. 29, 554.

De Jeude Collection, The Hague, 1735? (Hoet, I, p. 437).
De la Guiche Collection, 1771 (?).
Vassal de Saint-Hubert Collection, 1774 (?).
Dubarry Collection, 1774 (?).
De Lassay Collection, 1775 (?).
Lebrun Collection, 1792.
Sagan Collection.
Hohenzollern-Hechingen Collection at Loewenberg, 1881.
Herr Ed. F. Weber's collection, Hamburg. (N° in Catalogue, 212.)

(?) According to Smith, n° 66, the picture in these collections had *seven* figures.

AN OLD MAN ASLEEP BY THE FIRE

(ROYAL GALLERY, TURIN)

AN OLD MAN ASLEEP BY THE FIRE

(ROYAL GALLERY, TURIN)

An old man is seated to the right in a poorly furnished interior, by a large fire-place. His features are those of Rembrandt's father. His legs are crossed, and he sleeps, his head resting on his right hand. He wears a gray-brown cloak over a deep violet under-dress, and on his head a high, turban-like biretta. An earthenware vessel and a pair of tongs lie on the floor in front of the fire. A dead snipe hangs on the wall.

Small full-length figure.
Signed below with the monogram 𝓡𝓛 and dated *1629*.

Oak panel. H. 0ᵐ,5a; w. 0ᵐ,4t.

Etched (reversed) by A. Moitte in the Lebrun Gallery, as the work of Jan Lievens.

Bode, p. 368, 646; Dutuit, p. 37, n° 335; Wurzbach, n° 363.

Destouches Collection.
Lebrun Collection.
Royal Gallery, Turin. (N° in Catalogue, 377 bis). Ascribed to Jan Lievens.

THE SUPPER AT EMMAÜS

(MADAME ÉDOUARD ANDRÉ'S COLLECTION, PARIS)

THE SUPPER AT EMMAÜS

[MADAME ÉDOUARD ANDRÉ'S COLLECTION, PARIS]

Jesus sits at the table to the right, his figure shewing darkly against the strong light that falls on the wall from a candle concealed behind him. His face is in profile, the hair and beard almost black; his dress dark gray. In the dark foreground, in front of the table, one of the disciples, dressed in a dull, deep green tunic, with a girdle, has fallen on his knees before the Saviour in wondering adoration. An overturned stool lies to his left. Behind the table sits the other disciple, dressed in a dull yellowish brown tunic, open at the breast; he starts back in terror, gazing mutely at Jesus. On the table are a piece of roast meat, a silver bowl, and a few dishes. A serving-maid is busy in the background to the left, her dark figure relieved against the light.

Small full-length figures.
Signed in the lower right-hand corner with the monogram *RL*
Painted about 1629.

Paper on oak panel. H. 0ᵐ.37; w. 0ᵐ.41.

Dutuit, p. 19; Michel, pp. 155, 563.

W. Six Collection, 1734 ? (Hoet, I, p. 413.)
Leroy d'Etiolles Collection, Paris, 1861.
Sedelmeyer Collection, 1872.
Epstein Collection, Vienna, 1873.
Madame Édouard André's collection, Paris.

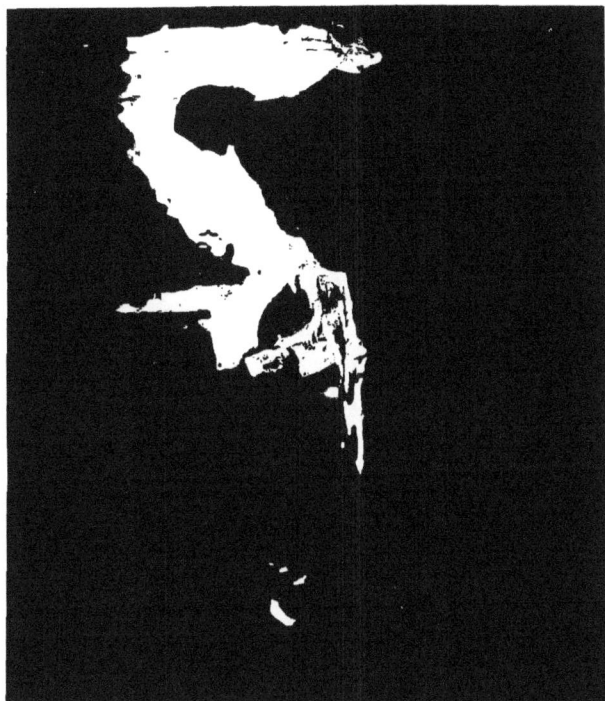

JUDAS BRINGING BACK
THE THIRTY PIECES OF SILVER

(BARON SCHICKLER'S COLLECTION, PARIS)

JUDAS BRINGING BACK THE THIRTY PIECES OF SILVER

BARON SCHICKLER'S COLLECTION. PARIS

In a spacious hall, supported in the middle by a column, Judas kneels before the High Priest's throne. He has cast the pieces of money on the floor, and wrings his hands in remorseful agony. His loose, brownish gray tunic, is thrown open, leaving his throat and breast bare. The High Priest, a seated figure in a dull red mantle embroidered with gold, a dull violet tunic girded with a scarf, and a light turban, turns away in disgust. Behind him stands another priest, in a menacing attitude, dressed in an Oriental robe of greenish blue, with a girdle of a deeper blue. Two Pharisees behind him to the right look on, half in pity. In the foreground to the left, a priest in a high cap and dull brown dress, seated, with his back to the spectator, at a table covered with a rug, and loaded with books, turns his head, and looks at the money. Three elders, in eastern garb of subdued tones, watch the scene in astonishment from behind him. On the column to the right of the High Priest, a polished steel shield hangs against a greenish curtain. Further in the background to the right, a staircase, with figures ascending.

Small full-length figures.

Signed on the step of the throne with the monogram $\mathcal{R}$ in very small characters, an apparently modern addition. There are traces of a larger monogram at the bottom of the picture, near the middle.

Painted about 1628 or 1629.

Canvas. H. 0m.77; w. 1m.01.

J. G. Van Vliet etched the figure of Judas in 1634. (Bartsch 22, a companion piece to Bartsch 21, see our plate 12.)

The picture is mentioned with high praise by Constantin Huygens, in a fragment of autobiography which breaks off abruptly in 1631. (See J. A. Worp in Oud Holland, IX. 1891, p. 126.) It is also mentioned in the Catalogue of the Gersaint Collection of Rembrandt's etchings, the compilers of which draw attention to the similarity of the Judas and the figure in Van Vliet's etching, Bartsch. 22.

A similar picture, engraved by Dunkarton when in the Fanshawe collection (Smith, VII, nᵒ 90 ; Vosmaer, 502), and now in the possession of Herr Wesendonck of Berlin, is not by Rembrandt, but by Salomon Koninck (exhibited at Berlin in 1890. Nᵒ in Cat. 64). A fairly exact contemporary copy in Mr. Henry Willett's collection at Brighton is probably by some pupil of Rembrandt's.

Young, in his " Tour in Ireland made in the years 1776, 1777 and 1778 and brought down to the end of the year 1779 ", speaks of having seen in Lord Charlemont's house in Dublin " some good pictures, particularly one by Rembrandt, of Judas throwing the money on the floor with a strong expression of guilt and remorse ; the whole group fine ".

Michel, pp. 60, 563.

M. G. Detsy Collection 1884 (as " School of Rembrandt ").

Haro Collection. Paris, 1892.

Martinet Collection, Paris, 1896.

Baron Schickler's collection, Paris.

REMBRANDT WITH DISORDERED HAIR

ROYAL GALLERY, CASSEL.

REMBRANDT WITH DISORDERED HAIR

(ROYAL GALLERY, CASSEL

At about the age of twenty-one, turned to the right, and looking straight in front of him. His brown locks hang in disorder about his head. A narrow linen collar falls over his brown doublet. A brilliant ray of sunshine penetrates above to the left, and lights up the lower portion of the right cheek and the throat. The upper part of the face is overshadowed by the hair, some strands of which are drawn with the butt-end of the brush in the impasto. Light-gray background.

Bust, about half life-size.
Painted about 1627-28

Oak panel. H. 0ᵐ,20; w. 0ᵇ,16.

Etched by J. Van Vliet in 1634, Bartsch 19.

Vosmaer, p. 122; Bode, p. 376. n° 59; Dutuit, p. 27. n° 123; Wurzbach, n° 50; Michel, pp. 31, 552.

Royal Gallery, Cassel. N° in Catalogue 208. Mentioned already in the inventory of 1749.

REMBRANDT(?) LAUGHING

(ROYAL GALLERY, THE HAGUE)

REMBRANDT (?) LAUGHING

ROYAL GALLERY, THE HAGUE)

Turned slightly to the left, his head to the right, he laughs roguishly at the spectator. Bare-headed, with dark brown, curly, disordered hair, and a slight beard. He wears a steel gorget over his brown doublet. A strong light falls from the left on the right side of the head, leaving the left in deep shadow. Broadly modelled in a fat impasto, with rich flesh tones, yellow and reddish lights, and greenish-blue shadows. Some strands of the hair drawn with the butt-end of the brush in the moist paint.

Head, half life-size.
Painted about 1629-30.

Copper, cradled. H. 0",154; w. 0",122. A band of wood about three centimetres wide encloses the copper, and is concealed under the frame.

Etched (reversed) by J. G. van Vliet on a slightly larger scale than the original (Bartsch 21) in a series dated 1630. The later states bear the inscription : *Heraklict.*

The compilers of the Hague Catalogue are of opinion that the person represented looks older than Rembrandt was in 1629-30. They suggest that the picture may be a study from Rembrandt's brother Adriaen Harmensz, his senior by ten years, to whom there is a strong likeness in this head.

Smith, n° 469; Vosmaer, p. 496; Dutuit, p. 19.

Munnicks van Cleef Collection, sold in Paris in 1864.
Charles de Boissière Collection, Paris, 1883 ("Ascribed to Rembrandt").
Langlois Collection, Paris.

Royal Gallery, The Hague. (N° in Catalogue, 598.)

REMBRANDT GAZING ENQUIRINGLY
AT THE SPECTATOR

(DUCAL MUSEUM, GOTHA)

REMBRANDT GAZING ENQUIRINGLY AT THE SPECTATOR

DUCAL MUSEUM, GOTHA.

The figure to the left, the face turned enquiringly to the spectator. The curly brown hair hangs in disorder about the face. A narrow crumpled collar lies over the dark doublet. Gray background. The light falls strongly from above on the lower part of the face, leaving the eyes in deep shadow.

Small bust, the hands not seen.
Signed to the right, above the chin, with the monogram *R* 1629.

Oak panel. H. 0ᵐ,18; w. 0ᵐ,14. A slip of wood about three centimetres wide is joined to the panel below.

Etched (reversed) by J. G. van Vliet, on a rather larger scale than the original, and dated 1634. Bartsch, n° 19.

Very closely akin to the autograph portrait, n° 208 in the Cassel Gallery.

The etching of 1633 (Bartsch, n° 17) deals with the same effect of light; the attitude is almost the same, though the costume differs a little from that of the picture, and the sitter wears a cap.

Vosmaer, pp. 122, 499; Bode, p. 377, n° 95; Dutuit. p. 29, n° 125; Wurzbach, n° 90; Michel, pp. 31, 553.

Ducal Museum, Gotha.

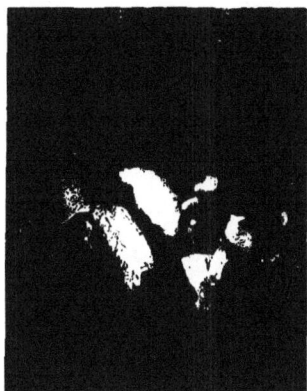

REMBRANDT WITH A BLACK CAP

(SIGNOR FERDINANDO MEAZZA'S COLLECTION. MILAN)

REMBRANDT WITH A BLACK CAP

SIGNOR FERDINANDO MEAZZA'S COLLECTION, MILAN.

Turned to the left, and looking straight before him. He wears a black cap on his curly brown hair, a dark gray doublet with a steel gorget, and a gold medallion on his breast. Light greenish gray background.

Small bust, the hands not seen.
Painted about 1629.

Oak panel. H. 0ᵐ.255; w. 0ᵐ.215 (original size. h. 0ᵐ.22; w. 0ᵐ.19).

Signor Ferdinando Meazza's collection, Milan.

REMBRANDT LAUGHING
WITH A CAP ON THE BACK OF HIS HEAD

(M. HENRI HEUGEL'S COLLECTION, PARIS)

REMBRANDT LAUGHING

WITH A CAP ON THE BACK OF HIS HEAD

(M. HENRI HEUGEL'S COLLECTION, PARIS

At about the age of twenty. Turned to the right, looking straight before him, and laughing. In a grayish brown doublet, shewing a small portion only of the shirt. A little black cap is pushed back, shewing his dark brown hair; he has a slight beard. Light, grayish brown background. The light falls full on the head from the left.

Bust, rather less than life-size, the hands not seen.
Signed with the monogram *RL*.

Oak panel. H. 0^m,41; w. 0^m,31.

In expression and attitude closely akin to the little etching, Bartsch n° 316.

A replica of this picture is in the possession of Count Estherhazy, at Nordkirchen, Westphalia. It is painted on an oak panel and measures 0^m40 in height by 0^m33 in width. It bears in the right hand top corner a monogram somewhat different from Rembrandt's usual signature. Bode, p. 380, n° 113; Dutuit, p. 41, n° 339; Wurzbach, n° 110; Michel, p. 554.

Sir Charles Robinson's collection, London.
M. Charles Sedelmeyer's collection, Paris.
M. Henri Heugel's collection, Paris.

REMBRANDT WITH A STEEL GORGET

(ROYAL GALLERY, THE HAGUE)

REMBRANDT WITH A STEEL GORGET

(ROYAL GALLERY, THE HAGUE)

Turned to the left, and looking straight before him; long, thick hair. He wears a dark doublet, with a steel gorget, over which lies a narrow crumpled linen collar. Grayish background, the light falling full from the left.

Bust, rather less than life-size.
Painted about 1629 or 1630.

Oak panel. H. 0ᵐ, 475; w. 0ᵐ.39.

Etched in reverse by Rembrandt himself, Bartsch 318, dated 1629. There is a study for the picture and the etching in the British Museum.

Scraped in mezzotint in 1775 by Valentine Green as *Prince Rupert*. The inscription on the plate states that the original belonged at the time to Mr. Orme of London, whereas the Hague picture was then in the Stadhouder's possession.

Engraved by Chataignier after Moreau for the *Musée Napoléon*, n° 29, and there ascribed to H. (sic) van Vliet. Engraved by Massard the elder after a drawing by Dubois, for the *Musée Français*, the text of which mentions the original as possibly by Van Vliet, and asserts that it was restored to the Prince of Hesse-Cassel in 1815. As, however, the measurements of the picture in question are given as two feet three inches, by two feet nine inches, the writer cannot possibly refer to this work.

There is a replica in the Germanic Museum at Nuremburg. It is of the same size, and below, to the right, bears a genuine monogram ℞ , and traces of the date (1629?). It seems probable, therefore, that this replica was at least painted under Rembrandt's own supervision, and that he himself touched it up. See the controversy as to the genuineness of this picture in the *Zeitschrift für bildende Kunst*, 1875, X. p. 381, 1876, XI. pp. 125, 222, 1877, XII, p. 32; and Dʳ Hofstede de Groot in *Verslagen omtrent s'Ryks Verzamelingen van Geschiedenis en Kunst*, 1893, XVI, p. 53. Vosmaer, p. 89; Bode, p. 378, n° 114; Dutuit, p. 31, n° 124, Michel, p. 554.

Smith, n° 243; Vosmaer, p. 89, 486; Bode, p. 378, n° 13, Dutuit, p. 36, n° 126; Wurzbach, n° 340; Michel, pp. 52, 565.

G. van Slingelandt Collection, The Hague, where it is known to have been in 1752. (Hoet II, p. 404.)

The Stadhouder William V's collection, from 1768.
From 1795-1815 in the Louvre.
Royal Gallery, The Hague. N in Catalogue, 148.

-- 66

REMBRANDT IN A MORNING GOWN

COUNT JULIUS ANDRASSY'S COLLECTION. BUDA-PESTH

REMBRANDT IN A MORNING GOWN

COUNT JULIUS ANDRASSY'S COLLECTION, BUDA-PESTH

The head turned to the front, the figure somewhat to the left. He wears a dark morning gown. Bare-headed, the thick curly brown hair in disorder. The coarsely treated features by no means attractive. The light falls full on the fair complexioned face.

Bust, life-size, the hands not seen.
Signed to the left above the chin with the monogram *R* 1630.

Oak panel. H. 0',49; w. 0'',39

It bears a resemblance to the small etching, Bartsch n° 4.

Michel, p. 559.

Purchased about forty years ago at a public sale in London.
Count Julius Andrassy's collection, Buda-Pesth.

REMBRANDT IN A PLUMED CAP

(MRS. JOHN L. GARDNER'S COLLECTION, BOSTON)

REMBRANDT IN A PLUMED CAP

(MRS JOHN L. GARDNER'S COLLECTION, BOSTON)

Full-face, the figure turned slightly to the right; he wears a violet cap with a high upright feather, a scarf of gold-embroidered brocade, and a yellowish green costume; round his neck a gold chain, from which hangs a medallion. The hair curly and luxuriant. A strong light falls from the left, above, on the lower part of the face, and the shoulder.

Half-length, life-size.
Signed to the right, about half way up the panel, with the monogram ℛ 1629.

Oak panel. H. 0ᵐ.885; w. 0ᵐ.735.

Engraved by R. Cooper (according to Smith, n° 445)

Smith, n° 422 (?) and 445. Dutuit, p. 17.

Duke of Buckingham's collection, Stowe House. Sold in London, 1848.
Sold among the pictures of an anonymous collection in London, July 13, 1895. Bought by Messrs P. and D. Colnaghi, London.
Mrs. John L. Gardner's collection, Boston.

PORTRAIT OF REMBRANDT'S MOTHER

SMALL SIZE

(Dr. A. BREDIUS' COLLECTION, THE HAGUE)

PORTRAIT OF REMBRANDT'S MOTHER
SMALL SIZE

(Dr. A. BREDIUS' COLLECTION, THE HAGUE)

In profile, to the right, the face turned slightly to the spectator, the eyes looking downwards. In a black dress and cap, both trimmed with fur. A long, parti-coloured veil is fastened above her forehead with an ornament, in which is a red stone. A white ruffle round the throat. Light-gray background. The light, which is evenly distributed, falls from the left, above.

Small bust, the hands not seen.
Painted about 1628.

Oak panel. H. 0",17; w. 0",13.

Exhibited at the Hague in 1890.

A contemporary replica was in the possession of Messrs. P. and D. Colnaghi in 1895.

There are old copies in the Brunswick Museum and in Prince Salm-Salm's collection at Anholt, the former ascribed to Eeckhout.

N° 20 (in the Ferdinandeum at Innsprück) is probably the pendant to this picture, and not the portrait at Nantes, as Michel supposes.

Michel, pp. 42, 565.

Fransen Collection, sold at Rotterdam, 1890 (described in the sale catalogue as a work in the manner of Gerard Dou).

Dr. A. Bredius' collection, The Hague; lent by the owner to the Royal Gallery, The Hague. (N° in Catalogue, 556.)

REMBRANDT'S FATHER AS " PHILO THE JEW "

(FERDINANDEUM, INNSBRUCK)

REMBRANDT'S FATHER AS "PHILO THE JEW"

(FERDINANDEUM, INNSPRÜCK)

Facing the spectator, his head slightly turned to the left. He has a short, thin beard, and wears a dark mantle with a broad collar of brown fur. His high, dark, bluish cap, is bound to his head with a brownish drapery. Light grayish-brown background. The light falls from above to the left.

Small bust. the hands not seen.
Signed with the monogram *Rl.*, *1630*.

Oak panel. H. o^m,215; w. o^m,17.

Etched (reversed) by J. G. van Vliet in 1633, on the same scale as the original, Bartsch n° 24. Copy by Dietricy in the Schleissheim Gallery, n° 773.

Smith, n° 361; Vosmaer, p. 487; Bode, 380, n° 100; Dutuit. p. 33, n° 358; Wurzbach, n° 380; Michel, pp. 44, 560.

Hope Collection. Formerly in an English collection.
Ferdinandeum, Innsprück. N° in Catalogue 599. Bequeathed by Tschager in 1856.

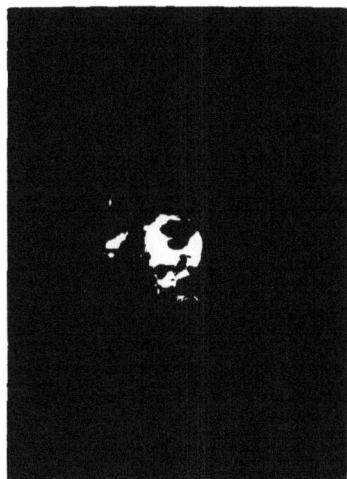

REMBRANDT'S MOTHER
IN A BLACK HOOD

(MR. ARTHUR SANDERSON'S COLLECTION, EDINBURGH)

REMBRANDT'S MOTHER IN A BLACK HOOD

(MR. ARTHUR SANDERSON'S COLLECTION, EDINBURGH)

Facing the spectator, in a large black hood, the wings of which fall upon her brown dress. At the throat a small portion of a white chemisette, in which is an ornament drawn with the butt-end of the brush. Her eyes are slightly downcast. The light falls upon her from the left. Light-greenish background.

Bust, life-size.
Painted about 1630.

Oak panel. H. o^m,35; w. o^m,29

Closely akin to the etching by Rembrandt, Bartsch n° 352.

Mr. Arthur Sanderson's collection, Edinburgh.

REMBRANDT'S MOTHER READING

REMBRANDT'S MOTHER READING

EARL OF PEMBROKE'S COLLECTION, WILTON HOUSE)

Seated, turned to the left, stooping over a large open book, which lies on her lap (or on a table before her?). She wears gold-rimmed glasses, and on her head a wide purple velvet-hood, which falls on her shoulders behind. Brownish gown, shewing the fastening of the pleated chemisette at the throat. Dark gray under-dress. Light gray background.

Nearly full-length, rather less than life-size.
Below to the left the unusual signature : *Rembrant P.*
Painted about 1629.

Canvas. H. o".75; w. o".61.

Bode, p. 381, n° 263; Dutuit, p. 47, n° 118; Wurzbach, n° 233; Michel, pp. 40, 559.

Earl of Pembroke's collection. Wilton House.

REMBRANDT'S MOTHER
AS THE PROPHETESS ANNA

(GRAND-DUCAL GALLERY, OLDENBURG)

REMBRANDT'S MOTHER AS THE PROPHETESS ANNA

(GRAND-DUCAL GALLERY, OLDENBURG)

Seated in an arm-chair, three-quarters to the right. On her lap lies a large open Bible, from which she reads. Her right hand is laid upon the page, her left is unseen. She wears a purplish red, fur-lined mantle, and on her head a cap of gold brocade, bound with a many-coloured Oriental scarf. Grayish background. A strong light falls from the left on the book, whence it is reflected on the face.

Nearly full-length, rather less than life-size.
Signed with the monogram *R* 1631.

Oak panel. H. 0m.60; w. 0m.48.

Etched (reversed) by J. G. van Vliet, Bartsch n° 18; and by L. Kühn, in Bode's "Bilderlese aus kleineren Gemäldesammlungen Deutschlands".

Smith, n° 592; Vosmaer, pp. 105, 490; Bode, p. 381, n° 115; Dutuit, p. 31, n° 119; Wurzbach, n° 112; Michel, pp. 40, 554.

The Elector of Saxony's Collection, sold at Amsterdam in 1765. (Terwesten, p. 443.)
Schonborn Collection, Pommersfelden, sold in Paris, 1867.
Grand-Ducal Gallery, Oldenburg. (N° in Catalogue, 192.)

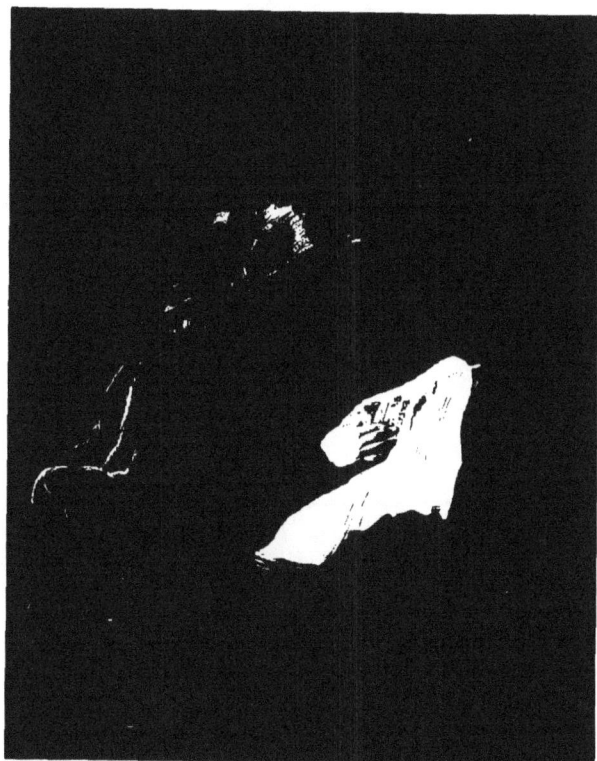

REMBRANDT'S MOTHER
WITH A LARGE HEAD-COVERING

REMBRANDT'S MOTHER WITH A LARGE HEAD-COVERING

(WINDSOR CASTLE

Standing, and turning to the right, her eyes turned in the same direction, and slightly downcast. She wears on her head a dark purple drapery, lined with gold brocade, which falls over her fur-lined mantle behind. A closely fitting white collar fastens under her chin. Dark-gray background. The sunlight falls on the head from above, to the right.

Bust, nearly life-size, the hands not seen.
Painted about 1630-31.

Oak panel. H. 0ᵐ,50; w. 0ᵐ,35, approximately.

Bode, p. 582, n° 26; Dutuit, p. 335, n° 120; Wurzbach, n° 142; Michel, pp. 40, 559.

H. M. The Queen's collection, Windsor Castle.

REMBRANDT'S FATHER GAZING FIXEDLY AT THE SPECTATOR

(DR. MELVILLE WASSERMANN'S COLLECTION, PARIS)

REMBRANDT'S FATHER

GAZING FIXEDLY AT THE SPECTATOR

DR. MELVILLE WASSERMANN'S COLLECTION, PARIS]

Slightly to the right, the face turned full to the spectator, and gazing fixedly at him. On the head a skull-cap, pushed far back. The toothless mouth firmly compressed; slight moustache and beard. Fur-trimmed cloak, shewing the shirt in front. A double gold chain with a medallion, across the breast. Dark background. Strongly illuminated from the left.

Small bust, the hands not seen.
Painted about 1630.

Oak panel. H. 0m,27 ; w. 0m,22.

Etched by Jan Lievens, Bartsch n° 21; afterwards copied by some other pupil of Rembrandt's, who added a lock of hair on the forehead. This latter plate was retouched by the master in 1637, and is the so-called First Oriental Head, Bartsch n° 286.

Michel, pp. 44, 558.

The Rev. Hugh Hutton's collection, Round Cottage, Edgebaston.
Mr. Humphry Ward's collection, London, 1892.
M. Ch. Sedelmeyer's collection, Paris.
Dr. Melville Wassermann's collection, Paris.

REMBRANDT'S FATHER

SMALL SIZE

(MUNICIPAL MUSEUM, NANTES)

REMBRANDT'S FATHER

SMALL SIZE

MUNICIPAL MUSEUM, NANTES)

The bald head turned three-quarters to the right.

Bust, about a quarter of life-size, the hands not seen.
Painted about 1629.

Oak panel. H. 0m,17½; w. 0m,14.

Émile Michel (page 42) is probably mistaken in asserting this picture to be the pendant to Dr Bredius' small portrait of Rembrandt's Mother, exhibited in the Hague Gallery.

There is a replica, with slight variations, in the Tours Museum which M. Durand-Gréville pronounces the original. See " L'Artiste ", June, 1896, and " Gazette des Beaux-Arts ", October and November, 1896, with reproductions.

Michel, pp. 42, 562.

The Duc de Feltre's Collection, 1852.
Municipal Museum, Nantes.   N° in Catalogue 522.)   Ascribed to J.-G. van Vliet.

REMBRANDT'S FATHER IN A PLUMED CAP

(THE HERMITAGE, ST. PETERSBURG)

REMBRANDT'S FATHER IN A PLUMED CAP

Full-face, the figure turned slightly to the left. Small moustache and chin-tuft, pearl earrings, black biretta with two dark gray feathers, a black cloak over the gray doublet. Steel gorget, a gaily coloured neckcloth, and a gold chain with an ornament. The back ground rather light.

Bust, rather less than lifesize, the hands not seen.
Signed above the shoulder to the right with the monogram *R*.
Painted about 1630.

Oak panel. Octagonal. H. 0°,36: w. 0°,27

Etched by Massaloff.

Vosmaer, p. 487: Bode, p. 179, n° 338; Dutuit, p. 37, n° 241. Wurzbach, n° 404; Michel, pp. 43, 567.

Acquired by the Empress Catherine II.
The Hermitage, S.t Petersburg. (N° in Catalogue 814.)

REMBRANDT'S FATHER
IN A CAP WITH A BLUE FEATHER

(MR. W. B. CHAMBERLIN'S COLLECTION, BRIGHTON)

REMBRANDT'S FATHER IN A CAP
WITH A BLUE FEATHER

(MR. W. B. CHAMBERLIN'S COLLECTION, BRIGHTON)

To the left, facing the spectator, but looking slightly to the left. Short grizzled beard. A dark doublet, with a polished steel gorget, shewing the collar above. A blue ostrich feather is fastened into the black cap by a gold chain. Rather a light gray background.

Bust, nearly life-size, the hands not seen.

Signed above, to the right, *Rembrandt f.* This signature is partly effaced, shewing traces of an earlier signature beneath.

Painted about 1630.

Oak panel. H. 0ᵐ,65: w. 0ᵐ,51.

There is an old copy in the Rijksmuseum at Amsterdam, where it passes as an original work. In 1808 it was in the National Museum at the Hague as a portrait of Willem van der Mark, Count of Lumey. Exhibited at the Royal Academy, 1884.

Michel, p. 557.

Mr. William Whitting Ashcroft's Collection till 1877(¹).
Sir Henry Bate Dudley's collection. Ely(¹).
Mr. W. B. Chamberlin's collection, Brighton.

1. In these collections the picture was described as a portrait of Willem van der Mark, Lord of Lumey.

REMBRANDT'S FATHER
IN A BROAD-BRIMMED HAT

(MR. W. A. BEERS' COLLECTION, NEW YORK)

REMBRANDT'S FATHER IN A BROAD-BRIMMED HAT

(MR. W. A. BEERS' COLLECTION, NEW YORK)

The figure turned slightly to the left, the head and the eyes to the right. In a dark purple mantle; over it a gold chain with a medallion, and a small, closely fitting steel gorget. A pearl earring in the right ear. He has a short grizzled beard, and curly hair. On his head a broad-brimmed black cap, with two dark ostrich feathers.

Bust, nearly life-size, the hands not seen.
Painted about 1631.

Canvas. H. 0m,75; w. 0m,62.

Bode, p. 413, n° 217; Dutuit, p. 43; Wurzbach, n° 156; Michel pp. 44, 557, 561.

Beresford Hope Collection, London, 1886.
M. Ch. Sedelmeyer's collection, Paris, 1887.
Mr W. H. Beers' collection, New York.

REMBRANDT'S FATHER IN A FUR CLOAK

(DR. A. BREDIUS' COLLECTION, THE HAGUE)

REMBRANDT'S FATHER IN A FUR CLOAK

(DR. A. BREDIUS' COLLECTION, THE HAGUE)

The figure slightly to the left, the face and eyes turned to the spectator. He wears a scanty gray beard. The dark brown cloak with a fur collar is open in front, shewing the dark under-dress and a bit of the shirt at the throat. The steel-blue cap was an after-thought of the master's. An under-paint, which has come through on the forehead, has the effect of a thin golden net-work. A strong light falls from above to the left on the right side of the head. The dark background is somewhat lighter on the right.

Bust, nearly life-size, the hands not seen.
Painted about 1629.

Oak panel. H. 0ᵐ,17; w. 0ᵐ,39.

Etched (reversed) by Rembrandt himself, in 1630. Bartsch. n° 304.

Michel, p. 44.

Mrs. Harrison's collection, Sutton Place, 1892.
Dr. A. Bredius' collection, The Hague. Lent by the owner to the Hague Gallery. (N° in Catalogue 567.)

REMBRANDT'S FATHER
IN A MORNING GOWN

(ROYAL GALLERY, CASSEL)

REMBRANDT'S FATHER IN A MORNING GOWN

(ROYAL GALLERY, CASSEL)

The figure to the left, the face turned with a lively gaze on the spectator. A black skull-cap on the bald head; scanty beard. The dark doublet is high at the throat, shewing only a narrow strip of the shirt. Grayish brown robe, faintly illuminated by the light, which falls from above to the left full on the head.

Bust, life-size, the hands not seen.

Painted about 1631.

Oak panel. H. 0ᵐ,48; w. 0ᵐ,37.

Etched (reversed) by Rembrandt as a half-length in 1631, the eyes cast down, and a fur cap on the head. Bartsch, nᵒ 263.

Michel, pp. 45, 552.

Von Friesen Collection, Dresden, sold at Cologne in 1885.
Habich Collection, Cassel, 1891.
Royal Gallery, Cassel.

AN OLD MAN
WITH A GOLD CROSS ON HIS BREAST

(ROYAL GALLERY, CASSEL)

AN OLD MAN WITH A GOLD CROSS ON HIS BREAST

(ROYAL GALLERY, CASSEL)

Facing the spectator, but turning and looking a little to the left. With a short gray beard; a black cap on his white hair. An ample black velvet mantle conceals all but a small portion of the gray doublet at the breast, on which hangs a double gold chain with a large cross. Brownish background. The light from the left above plays over the head.

Bust, nearly life-size, the hands not seen.
Signed to the right, half way up the panel : $\mathcal{R}$ 1639.

Oak panel. Octagonal. H. 0m,66; w. 0m,56.

Etched by W. Unger.

Vosmaer, pp. 88, 486; Bode, p. 381, n° 70; Dutuit, p. 27, n° 357; Wurzbach, n° 58; Michel, p. 552.

Royal Gallery, Cassel. (N° in Catalogue 209.) The principal inventory of 1749 (n° 3) shews it to have been in the Cassel Gallery at that date.

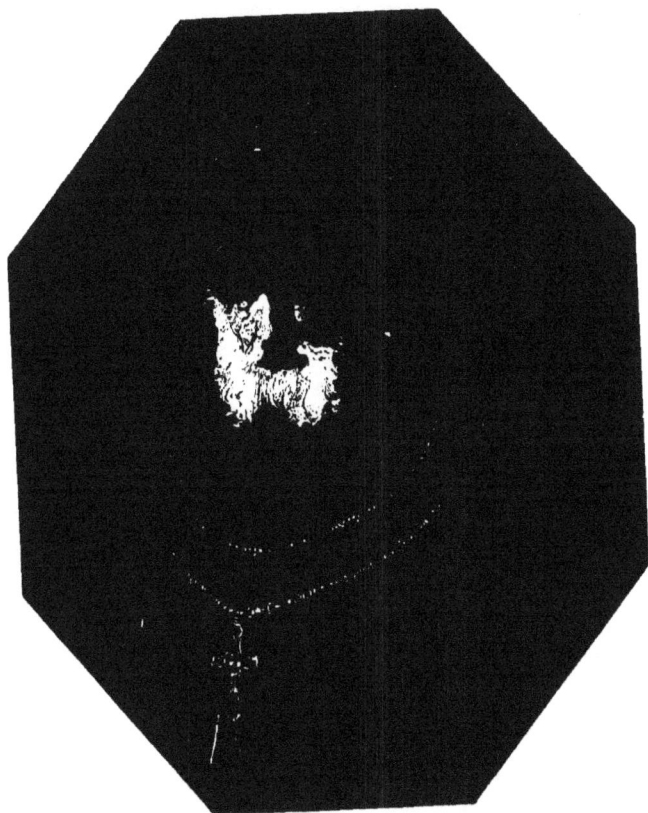

PORTRAIT OF AN OLD MAN
WITH A BRISTLY BEARD

(SIGNOR E. P. FABBRIS COLLECTION, FLORENCE)

PORTRAIT OF AN OLD MAN WITH A BRISTLY BEARD

(SIGNOR E. P. FABBRI'S COLLECTION, FLORENCE)

An aged man, with a thick, bristly white beard, his head slightly inclined to his left shoulder. He faces the spectator, and looks straight before him. A dark violet cap striped with gold is fastened on one side of his head. He wears a dark gray doublet with a broad gold edging. Some strands of the beard drawn in the moist paint with the butt-end of the brush. Dark gray background.

Bust, life-size.
Painted about 1629.

Oak panel. H. 0ᵐ,59; w. 0ᵐ,47.

The Marquis of Cholmondeley's collection, London, 1886.
M. Ch. Sedelmeyer's collection, Paris, 1887.
Signor E. P. Fabbri's collection, Florence.

ST. PAUL WRITING HIS EPISTLE
TO THE THESSALONIANS

(M. J. H. HARJES' COLLECTION, PARIS)

ST. PAUL WRITING HIS EPISTLE
TO THE THESSALONIANS

(M. J. H. HARJES' COLLECTION, PARIS)

Seated in an arm-chair at a table, from which he turns away, looking straight before him, and facing the spectator. Long gray beard and hair; loose gray robe. He holds a pen in his right hand, resting his elbow upon the table, on the dull green cover on which lie some manuscripts. At the top of the second Epistle to the Thessalonians, which the Apostle is writing, the following words are distinctly legible; Ἐρωτῶμεν δὲ ὑμᾶς ἀδελφοὶ ὑπὲρ τῆς παρουσίας τοῦ κυρίου ἡμῶν Ἰησοῦ Χριστοῦ καὶ ἡμῶν ἐπισυναγωγῆς ἐπ᾽ αὐτόν [1]. Pale gray background. Subdued light.

Three-quarters length, life-size.
Signed to the left of the manuscript : *Remb...*
Painted about 1609-70.

Canvas, H. 1m.08; w. 0m.98.

Exhibited at the Royal Academy in 1871.

Bode, p. 426, n° 206; Dutuit, p. 44, n° 100; Wurzbach, n° 183; Michel, p. 557.

Van Schuylenburch Collection. The Hague, 1735 (?) [?].
Meulan Collection, 1778 (?).
Lord Dudley's collection, sold in London, 1892.
M. Ch. Sedelmeyer's collection, Paris, 1892.
M. J. H. Harjes' collection, Paris.

1. II Thes., II, 1.
2. Een overheerlijk kragtig en schoon Stuk door Rynbrand van Ryn, verbeeldende den Apostel Paulus, niet minder als van Dutuit. H. 3 F. 2 Z. Br. 3. F. ¡ 1/2 Z. 150 Gld. Hoet I, p. 557.

ST. PAUL SEATED AT A WRITING-TABLE
AND MEDITATING

(IMPERIAL GALLERY, VIENNA)

ST. PAUL SEATED AT A WRITING-TABLE
AND MEDITATING

(IMPERIAL GALLERY, VIENNA)

The Apostle, an aged man with luxuriant white hair and beard, is seated at a writing-table on which lies an open folio, with a sheet of paper upon it. He has paused in his writing, and gazes meditatively before him. His left arm rests on the book, his right on the back of the chair. He holds his pen in his right hand. Over his dull yellow tunic he wears a pale bluish robe, held together by a gaily coloured Oriental scarf. On the table, a dull blue cover with a wide gold border. A two-handed sword hangs against the wall in the background, behind some books.

> Three-quarters length, life-size.
> Painted about 1636.
> The old signature, *Rembrandt f.* 1636, mentioned by Mechel and Krafft, is almost cleaned away. Its authenticity was doubtful. The date, 1636, must, if, indeed, it was genuine, have been misread in mistake for 1630. Th. von Frimmel, in his *Kl. Galeriestudien*, N. F. I., p. 77, erroneously states it to be a work contemporary with the " Syndics ".

> Canvas. H. 1m.26; w. 1m.10.

> The authenticity of this picture is erroneously called in question by Mechel in the Catalogue of 1783, by Rosa in the Catalogue of 1796, and by Eduard von Engerth in the official Catalogue of 1884.
> Etched by W. Unger for the " Imperial Gallery of Vienna". (In Lützow's descriptive text for this work, the ascription to Rembrandt is contested.)
> Rembrandt's large etching (Bartsch, 149). and the red chalk drawing in the Louvre for it, are both closely akin to this picture.

> Vosmaer, pp. 97, 512; Bode. pp. 426, n° 123; Dutuit, p. 33, n° 99; Wurzbach, p. 370; Michel, pp. 218, 560.

> It is known to have been in the Imperial Collection since 1718; mentioned in the inventory of the Castle of Prague (n° 452).

> Imperial Gallery, Vienna. (N° in Catalogue 1145.)

ST. PAUL SEATED AT A WRITING-TABLE AND MEDITATING

(MR. M. C. D. BORDEN'S COLLECTION, NEW YORK)

ST. PAUL SEATED AT A WRITING-TABLE
AND MEDITATING

In composition, almost identical with n° 35. There are, however, a few more books behind the table. The back of the chair is lighter in tone, and slightly different in position, the dark table-cover has no border, and local colour is more strictly subordinated to the prevailing grayish brown tone.

Three-quarters length, life-size.
Painted at the same time as the replica n° 35 , about 1630.

Canvas. H. 1m.18; w. 0m.95

Michel, p. 112 (English edition, vol. I, p. 111, 2).

Duke of Somerset's collection (known as the Stover Collection).
Thos. Agnew and Sons' collection, 1890.
Sir Charles Robinson's collection, London, 1892.
M. Charles Sedelmeyer's collection, Paris, 1894.
Mr. M. C. D. Borden's collection, New York.

1. The composition is an exact reproduction of that of a drawing in the Louvre, Lippmann, n° 158, from which Rembrandt etched the plate known as the " Old Man studying " (Vieillard, homme de lettres, B. 149). The plate is, however, reversed.

THE HOLY FAMILY
RESTING DURING THE FLIGHT INTO EGYPT

(MR. A. R. BOUGHTON KNIGHT'S COLLECTION, DOWNTON CASTLE)

THE HOLY FAMILY

RESTING DURING THE FLIGHT INTO EGYPT

MR. A. R. BOUGHTON KNIGHT'S COLLECTION, DOWNTON CASTLE.

The Holy Family rests at the base of a steep declivity, from which projects a massive withered tree-trunk. The Virgin, seated in the middle, is about to suckle the Babe in swaddling clothes on her lap. She wears a high felt cap over the kerchief on her head; a light flowered scarf hangs from her shoulders, and a speckled fur rug lies across her knees. Joseph, bare-headed, in a dark dress, crouches on the ground behind her to the left, absorbed in a book. In the extreme foreground, a rug, a gourd-flask, and a stick. From the tree stem above the Virgin hang the harness of the ass, and a flat basket-cradle. To the left, a view of a wooded landscape.

Small figures, whole length.
Signed : *Rembrandt.*
Painted about 1631.

Oak panel. H. o^m,77; w. o^m,60.

Mr. A. R. Boughton Knight's collection, Downton Castle.

THE HOLY FAMILY
IN THE CARPENTER'S SHOP

(ROYAL PINACOTHEK. MUNICH)

THE HOLY FAMILY IN THE CARPENTER'S SHOP

(ROYAL PINACOTHEK, MUNICH)

The Virgin is seated to the left, facing the spectator. She supports the sleeping Babe in swaddling clothes upon a fox-skin rug on her lap, and inclines her head to look at him. She is dressed in a pinkish-violet robe and transparent veil. In the foreground to the right, Joseph bends over the child's basket-cradle. He wears a dull green robe, open at the throat. A carpenter's tools hang against the wall; on the floor to the left, a pot and a billet of wood.

Full-length figures, life-size.
Signed below to the right : *Rembrandt f. 1631.*

Canvas. H. 1ᵐ,91; w. 1ᵐ,30.

Etched by P. Hahn.
There is a drawing of the composition in the Albertina at Vienna (n° 396).

Vosmaer, pp. 104, 489; Bode, p. 390, n° 103; Dutuit, p. 30, n° 36; Wurzbach, n° 99; Michel, pp. 78, 554.

Anonymous collection at Amsterdam in 1735 (?). (Hoet I, p. 442 : " ungemein herrlich ", II. 100.)
Brought to Munich in 1799 with other works from the Mannheim Gallery.
Royal Pinacothek, Munich. (N° in Catalogue 324.)

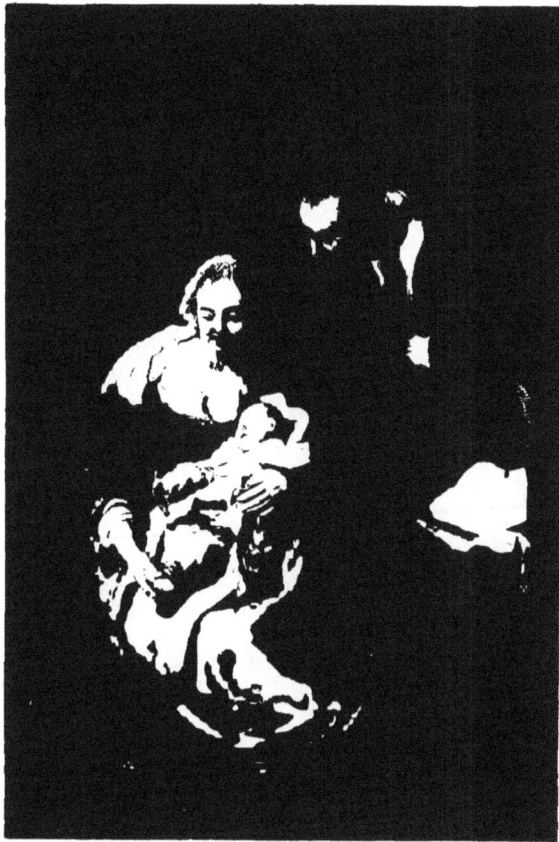

JEREMIAH MOURNING THE DESTRUCTION
OF JERUSALEM

(COUNT SERGEI STROGANOFF'S COLLECTION. ST. PETERSBURG)

JEREMIAH MOURNING THE DESTRUCTION OF JERUSALEM

(COUNT SERGEI STROGANOFF'S COLLECTION, ST. PETERSBURG)

The aged prophet is seated at the base of a pillar near the opening in a grotto, on a purplish red velvet drapery, with a wide blue border, embroidered with flowers. He rests his head on his left hand. Over his closely fitting tunic he wears a pale violet-blue mantle trimmed with fur. Near him to the right some vessels of gold, a large water-bottle, and a book, with the inscription " Bibel ". In the background to the left, a burning town, with soldiers and distracted citizens.

Small figure, full-length.
Signed in the middle of the panel at the bottom : *Qu* 1630.

Oak panel. H. 0m,58; w. 0m,46.

Etched by G. F. Schmidt, under the title " Lot ". (Wessely, n° 158.)

Smith, n° 9, 190; Vosmaer, pp. 87, 486; Bode, p. 384, n° 353; Dutuit, p. 54, n° 7; Wurzbach, n° 428; Michel, pp. 52, 567.

Cesar Collection, Berlin, 1768.
Count Sergei Stroganoff's collection, St. Petersburg.

ST. ANASTASIUS

(NATIONAL MUSEUM, STOCKHOLM)

The aged Father is seated somewhat in the background of a lofty vaulted room, behind a round table with a greenish cloth, absorbed in the study of a folio which lies on the table before him. He wears a long mantle of a subdued violet tone, fastened in front with cords; on his head, a red skullcap. His left hand is laid on the back of the chair. Near him to the right a high circular window with deep embrasure, from which the last warm rays of evening light stream into the room. Against the pillar behind the saint, a stone altar with a crucifix. Two curtains to the left are gathered back, shewing the inner portion of the cell[¹].

Small figure, full-length.
Signed on a sheet of parchment over the saint's head : *Rembrant ft. 1631.*

Oak panel. H. 0ᵐ,60; w. 0ᵐ,48.

Etched (reversed) by P. de Balliu (Bartsch, II. p. 119. n° 2); and by L. Lowenstam, in the *Tidskrift for bildande Konst,* 1883.
Engraved on wood by J. Peterson in the " Museum ", Stockholm, 1888.
The figure of the saint (reversed) is introduced in Rembrandt's upright plate " The Child Jesus among the Doctors of the Law ", Bartsch, n° 66.

Smith, n° 130; Vosmaer. p. 489; Bode, p. 385, n° 361; Dutuit. p. 40, n° 104; Wurzbach, n° 435; Michel, pp. 67, 567.

Van Eversdyck Collection, The Hague, 1766. (Terwesten, p. 533.)
Queen Louisa Ulrica's collection, n° 274.
King Gustavus III.'s collection.
National Museum, Stockholm. (N° in Catalogue 579.)

(¹) See *Zeitschrift für bildende Kunst,* XVII, pp. 52, 163. — *Repertorium für Kunstwissenschaft,* IV, p. 445. — *Athenæum,* 1878. — Supplement to the *Augsburg Allgemein. Zeitung,* March, 1878.

ST. PETER PENITENT

(PRINCE DE RUBEMPRÉ DE MÉRODE'S COLLECTION, BRUSSELS)

ST. PETER PENITENT

Saint Peter kneels on the ground near a pillar, his hands clasped in prayer, and gazes mournfully before him. He turns to the left, his face three-quarters to the front. He wears a dull brown over-dress and black tunic; his greenish gray mantle is behind him, to the right. Beside him lie his keys, and a bundle of straw for his bed. The kneeling figure is illumined by subdued sunlight. The sketchy, thinly painted background, is of a dull gray stone-colour.

Small figure, full-length.
Signed below, to the right *Rt 1631.*

Oak panel. H. 0ᵐ,78; w. 0ᵐ,33.

The composition was etched by G. F. Schmidt in 1770 as a work of Ferdinand Bol, and described as such in the Trible Collection at Berlin (Wessely, n° 170). It seems probable that the engraver worked from an old copy in possession of Count Lanckoronski.

Exhibited at the Corps legislatif, Paris, 1874, when it was erroneously described in the Catalogue as belonging to M. Ed. André's collection. Exhibited at Brussels in 1886.

Vosmaer, p. 489; Bode, p. 585, n° 288; Dutuit, p. 54, n° 96; Wurzbach, n° 290.

Prince de Chalais' collection, Paris.
Prince de Rubempré de Mérode's collection, Brussels.

HIGH PRIEST WITH A BOOK

(M. ALBERT LEHMANN'S COLLECTION, PARIS)

HIGH PRIEST WITH A BOOK

M. ALBERT LEHMANN'S COLLECTION. PARIS

Standing, and turning to the right, almost in profile. He has a full gray beard, and holds an open folio in his hands. His dress is a rich and fanciful priestly costume : a long white tunic with wide sleeves, and over it a light, gold-embroidered mantle fastened in front with a clasp. A long veil hangs behind him from the helmet-shaped mitre with golden ornaments on his head. To the right, an octagonal table with a grayish green cover, on which stands a silver ewer; the pastoral staff rests against it; further behind, an arm-chair. In the background, to the left of the prophet, a curtain, apparently concealing a throne or altar.

Small figure, full-length.
Signed below, to the right : *Rembrandt f.*
Painted about 1631-1632.

Oak panel. H. 0ᵐ.58; w. 0ᵐ.575.

An old copy in the Schwerin Gallery, tentatively ascribed to Salomon Koninck, and entered in the Catalogue (n° 577) as " Zacharias beholding the Vision of the Angel Gabriel " is pronounced by Dr Hofstede de Groot a copy by Lievens after Rembrandt. See *Repertorium für Kunstwissenschaft*, XVII, p. 180.

The figure of this priest is introduced in Rembrandt's etching, the little " Circumcision ", Bartsch, n° 48. There, however, he holds the staff in his hand, and smoke issues from the vessel on the table.

Smith, n° 145.

Jer. Harman's collection, England, 1844.
Captain E. Purvis' collection, 1875.
M. Charles Sedelmeyer's collection, Paris.
M. Albert Lehmann's collection, Paris.

THE SAVANT

(DUCAL GALLERY, BRUNSWICK

THE SAVANT

DUCAL GALLERY, BRUNSWICK)

Seated to the left, at a table, absorbed in what he is reading, his head supported on his left hand. He wears a small black cap, and, over his dark brown under-dress, a black sleeveless robe, shewing the shirt at throat and wrists. The table is covered with a dull steel-blue cloth with a green flowered border, on which are various large books in brown bindings, some of them resting against a book-case with a green curtain. Light grayish green wall.

Small figure, full-length
To the left, traces of the signature and date : R... 3 (probably *R* 1631).

Oak panel. H.0",51; w. 0",44.

Its authenticity has been erroneously called in question by H. Riegel (*Beitrage*, II, 236) and others

Etched by W. Unger.

Vosmaer, p. 498; Bode, p. 587, n° 47; Dutuit, p. 26, n° 569, Wurzbach, n° 17; Michel, p. 552.

Ducal Collection, Salzdahlum.
Ducal Gallery, Brunswick. (N° in catalogue 234.)

SIMEON IN THE TEMPLE

(ROYAL GALLERY, THE HAGUE)

SIMEON IN THE TEMPLE

(ROYAL GALLERY, THE HAGUE)

The interior of a lofty Gothic cathedral. In the foreground, to the right of the centre, kneels the aged Simeon, draped in a flowing mantle of golden brocade, and holding the Infant Christ in his arms. Near him, the Virgin, in a light blue robe and veil; she also kneels, her eyes fixed on the Child. To the left, and rather more in the foreground, stands the High Priest, his back nearly turned to the spectator, his hands uplifted in benediction. He wears a long, deep purple mantle, and a many-coloured head-dress. Around the group, several old men, among them Joseph, kneeling, the dove in his hand. In the immediate foreground, two old men, seated. In the background to the right, a wide and lofty staircase, on which are various figures. At its summit, the canopied throne of the High Priest.

Signed below, to the right Rt 1631.

Oak panel. H. 0^m,60; w. 0^m,48.

An arched slip, 13 centimetres high, added to the panel in the eighteenth century, to make it uniform in shape with Gerard Dou's " Young Housekeeper ", is now concealed by the frame.

There are several hasty charcoal sketches for this picture in the Print Room of the Old Pinacothek at Munich. N° 1394 in the Dresden Gallery is an old copy of the work by Willem de Poorter.

Engraved by J. de Frey for the " Musée francais "; by Devilliers ainé after a drawing by Plonski for the " Musée Napoléon "; in aquatint by Bierweiler; in outline by Heydeloff in the " Steengracht Gallery "; lithographed by G. C. A. Last in the " Desguerrois Gallery ", and by J. D. Steuerwald in " Een Kunstpraatje "; chromo-lithographed by Spanier; engraved on wood by J. W. G. Zimmermann, and by Berthold (*).

So early as the year 1658, a " Simeon " by Rembrandt is mentioned in a legal document, though no particulars of the work are given (*Oud Holland*, VIII, p. 182).

Smith, n°^s 64 and 68; Vosmaer, pp. 101, 488; Bode, p. 390, n° 10; Dutuit, p. 36, n° 52; Wurzbach, n° 338; Michel, pp. 52, 565.

A. Bout Collection, The Hague, 1733. (Hoet I, 391.)
Collection at the Castle of Loo.
William V.'s collection.
In the Louvre from 1795-1815.
Royal Gallery, The Hague. (N° in Catalogue 145.)

(*) All these reproductions, with the exception of W. de Poorter's copy, have the arched top.

THE RAISING OF LAZARUS

THE RAISING OF LAZARUS

(MR. CH. T. YERKES' COLLECTION, NEW YORK.)

Christ stands behind the open grave, upon the grave-stone, his right hand uplifted. He wears a loose robe of dull purple, and a brownish mantle across his left shoulder. Lazarus, still in the grave, slowly raises the upper part of his body in its white shroud, struggling back to life. In the immediate foreground to the left of the grave, a young woman in a deep green gown kneels in shadow. Behind her, an old man with a long black beard, in profile, dressed in a purplish red garment. To the left of Jesus, two men, and a young woman in green, bend eagerly forward to the grave; in the shadow to the right, five male heads may be distinguished. On the rocky wall to the right, the accoutrements of the dead man are hung above his grave : an Eastern sword and a quiver, both cased in red velvet, a bow and a turban.

Small figures, full-length.
Signed below, to the right : *Remb*....
Painted about 1630, before the famous etching (Bartsch, n° 73), which, although it has much in common with the picture, is greatly superior.

Oak panel. H. 0m,51; w. 0m,36.

In Rembrandt's inventory of the year 1656, a " Raising of Lazarus " is included. (Bovinski, n° 38.) A picture of the same subject also figures in the inventory of the Amsterdam dealer, Johannes de Renialme, in 1657. But, in this latter, we find the " Lascrus Verweckinge " valued at 600 guldens, a price so high, as compared with that of 1500 guldens allowed for the " Adulteress before Christ " (the National Gallery picture?), that we can scarcely suppose the picture in question to be identical with the early work above described. Its value in the seventeenth and eighteenth centuries would hardly have exceeded 20-30 gulden.

Engraved by Klauber. (When in the Duval Collection.)

Dutuit, p. 18; Michel, p. 564.

David Grenier Collection (?), Middelburg. 1712.
Sold by auction at Amsterdam, June 4, 1727 (?), Hoet. I. 316.
Lebrun Collection, 1811 (?).
Winckler Collection, Leipzig.
Duval Collection, Geneva, sold in London, 1846.
Comte de Morny's collection. 1852.
M. Ch. Sedelmeyer's collection, 1891.
Mr. Ch. T. Yerkes' collection, New York (formerly Chicago).

DAVID PLAYING THE HARP BEFORE SAUL

(STAEDEL INSTITUTE, FRANKFORT ON THE MAIN)

DAVID PLAYING THE HARP BEFORE SAUL

(STAEDEL INSTITUTE, FRANKFORT ON THE MAIN)

Saul is seated on a low chair in the foreground to the right, in front of a wide curtain. He gazes fixedly before him, apparently in deep agitation, and clutches a javelin in his right hand. A reddish velvet mantle, adorned with a gold chain, partly conceals his long dull blue robe, bordered with gold; a golden pheasant is fastened into his gaily coloured turban. Behind the king, a curtain, almost neutral in colour, and near him to the left, a table with a green cloth; in the shadow to the left kneels the youthful David with his harp, by the music of which he seeks to charm Saul's melancholy.

Small figures, full-length.
Painted about 1630-1631.

Oak panel. H. 0m,62; w. 0m,50.

Engraved by W. de Leeuw (Bartsch, II, p. 131, n° 44).

Smith, n° 32; Bode, p. 431, n° 92; Dutuit, p. 29; n° 27; Wurzbach, n° 86; Michel, pp. 153, 553.

De Neufville-Gontard Collection, Frankfort on the Main, 1817.
Staedel Institute, Frankfort on the Main. (N° in Catalogue 183.) Formerly ascribed to Salomon Koninck.

DIANA BATHING

(M. E. WARNECK'S COLLECTION, PARIS)

DIANA BATHING

M. E. WARNECK'S COLLECTION, PARIS

Nude, but for a white cap on her head, her face turned to the spectator. She sits on the bank, her shirt under her, her feet in the water, resting her arms on the cherry-coloured velvet robe with gold embroideries which lies at the base of a tree beside her. Her quiver and arrows are above it, her bow lies on the ground to the right. Dark background to the right, and from the same side, a strong light, equally diffused over the naked body.

Small figure, full-length.
Painted about 1630-1631.

Oak panel. H. 0m,18; w. 0m,17.

Etched by Rembrandt himself on the same scale as the original. Bartsch, n° 201.

Duclos Collection, Paris.
Hulot Collection, Paris, 1892 (as a work of the school of Rembrandt).
M. E. Warneck's collection, Paris.

PORTRAIT OF A YOUNG LAD

HERR ADOLPH THIEM'S COLLECTION. SAN REMO

PORTRAIT OF A YOUNG LAD

About fifteen years old. Turned to the left, and looking sullenly at the spectator, his lips closely compressed. He wears a brownish purple doublet, with a small linen collar turned over it. Bareheaded, with short, brownish hair. A strong light from the left falls on the head and the collar; the left side of the head is in deep shadow. Gray background, lighter near the head to the right.

Bust, rather less than life-size, the hands not seen.
Signed below to the right with the monogram: *Ra*
Painted about 1629-1630.

Oak panel. H. 0m.45; m. 0m.35.

Bode, p. 579, n° 166; Dutuit, p. 48, n° 240; Michel, p. 556.

Earl of Poulett's collection, Hinton House.
M. Ch. Sedelmeyer's collection, Paris.
Herr Adolph Thiem's collection, San Remo (formerly at Berlin).

A YOUNG MAN IN A TURBAN

(WINDSOR CASTLE)

A YOUNG MAN IN A TURBAN

(WINDSOR CASTLE)

The figure turned to the left, the beardless face confronting the spectator. An ample turban of neutral tones, fastened together with a golden clasp, is bound tastefully about his head. Over his dark doublet, he wears an Oriental shawl of subdued tints, and on his breast a broad gold chain. Dark background. A strong light from the left falls on the right half of the head.

Bust, almost life-size; the hands not seen.
Signed below to the right: *R* *1631*.

Oak panel, H. 0m,50; w. 0m,40.

Erroneously described by Emile Michel as a portrait of the painter Gerard Dou. Exhibited at Manchester, 1857.

Vosmaer, pp. 105, 489; Bode, n° 264; Dutuit. p. 33; n° 242; Wurzbach, n° 141; Michel, pp. 46, 559; Waagen II, 430; Bürger, *Trésors d'Art*, p. 246.

Her Majesty the Queen's collection, Windsor Castle.

PORTRAIT OF A SAVANT
(THE SO-CALLED PORTRAIT OF COPPENOL)

(THE HERMITAGE, ST. PETERSBURG)

PORTRAIT OF A SAVANT
(THE SO-CALLED PORTRAIT OF COPPENOL)

(THE HERMITAGE, ST. PETERSBURG)

A man of about forty years old, seated sideways to the left at a table; he pauses in his writing and looks round at the spectator. Still holding his pen, he rests both hands on a sheet of paper which lies on the open folio before him. A low desk stands on the table, which is covered with a greenish cloth with yellow pattern. The writer wears a black doublet and a wide ruff; his thick hair is cut short, his beard trimmed and pointed *à la Henri Quatre*. Dark background. The light falls into the foreground from the left.

Rather more than half-length, and nearly life-size.
Signed above to the right $\mathcal{R}$ *1631*.

Canvas. H. 1m,13; w. 0m.92.

Etched by Fithol in the " Brühl Gallery " and by Massaloff; lithographed by E. Huot.

Vosmaer, pp. 116, 493; Bode, p. 382, n° 132; Dutuit, p. 37, n° 205; Wurzbach, n° 399; Michel, pp. 116, 566.

Count Brühl's collection.
The Hermitage, St. Petersburg. (N° in Catalogue 808.) Purchased by Catherine II.

PORTRAIT OF NICOLAES RUTS

(MR. JOSEPH RUSTON'S COLLECTION, THE HAGUE)

PORTRAIT OF NICOLAES RUTS

(MR. JOSEPH RUSTON'S COLLECTION, LINCOLN)

A healthy, energetic-looking man, about fifty years old, with a short beard. He stands behind a purplish red leather chair, on the back of which he rests his right hand. Turning slightly to the left, he looks straight before him, holding up a letter in his left hand. A sleeveless violet mantle, lined and trimmed with fur, partly conceals his black doublet. He wears a large fur cap on his head, which is enframed in a broad gauffered ruff. Rather a light background. The light falls full on him from the left above.

Life-size, rather more than half-length.
Signed above to the right : *Rt 1631*.

Mahogany panel, H. 1ᵐ,17; w. 0ᵐ,88.

The title of this portrait is derived from the inscription on a drawing by A. Delfos in the collection of Dʳ C. W. J. J. Pape, of The Hague : " Het portret van Nicolaes Ruts, levensgroot door Rembrandt van Rijn 1632(?). A. Delfos 1799 thans by den heer Joost Romswinckel te Leiden ".
Engraved in outline by A. L. Zeelander for the " Gallery " of King William II. of Holland.

Vosmaer, pp. 490, 495; Bode, p. 382, n° 215; Dutuit, p. 45, n° 226; Wurzbach, n°ˢ 199, 446; Michel, p. 557.

Collection of Susannah Ruts, the widow of Joannes Boddens, married in 1636 to Pieter van der Hagen. (Prot. Not. L. Lamberti, Amsterdam.)
Joost Romswinckel Collection, Leyden, 1799.
Collection of the Queen of the Netherlands.
Collection of King William II., 1850.
Adrian Hope Collection, sold in London, 1894.
Mr. Joseph Ruston's collection, Lincoln.

PORTRAIT OF A YOUNG GIRL

(DR. A. BREDIUS' COLLECTION, THE HAGUE)

PORTRAIT OF A YOUNG GIRL

(DR. A. BREDIUS' COLLECTION, THE HAGUE)

About seventeen or eighteen years old, seated, facing the spectator, the figure turned slightly to the left. She wears a closely fitting black dress, a narrow gauffered ruff, and a white cap over her smooth, light brown hair. Brown eyes, fresh complexion. Light gray background. Strongly illuminated from the left.

Bust, rather less than life-size, the hands not seen.
Signed above to the right with the monogram (the cross stroke of the L is erased).
Painted about 1630-31.

Oak panel. H. 0″.565; w. 0″.455

The sitter seems also to have been the model for the small female figure in Herr James Simon's collection at Berlin.

Purchased in 1893 from Mr. Martin Colnaghi in London, where the picture was known among dealers as a work of Aelbert Cuyp.

Dr. A. Bredius' collection, The Hague. Lent by the owner to the Royal Gallery, The Hague. (N° in Catalogue. 577.)

A YOUNG GIRL, STANDING IN AN INTERIOR

(HERR JAMES SIMON'S COLLECTION, BERLIN)

A YOUNG GIRL, STANDING IN AN INTERIOR

(HERR JAMES SIMON'S COLLECTION, BERLIN)

About eighteen years old.   Looking straight before her, and turning almost full-face to the spectator, she enters a sunlit room through a door on the right, approached by a couple of steps.   She wears a wide ruff, a flat cap and cuffs, a black dress, with striped sleeves of purple and black, and holds up her skirt with her left hand, revealing a grayish under-dress through the opening in front.   To the left, a table with a reddish Smyrna rug, an open box upon it.   Behind it a chair with a green cover. In front of the table, quite to the left, a green curtain, drawn back.   To the left, behind the figure, a fluted pillar.

Small figure, full-length.
Painted about 1630.

Oak panel. Octagonal, the corners added. H. 0ᵐ,72; w. 0ᵐ,555.

The model seems to be the same as in Dʳ Bredius' bust portrait at The Hague (nᵒ 52).
Etched by Laguillermie for M. Ch. Sedelmeyer's sale catalogue.
Exhibited at Berlin in 1890.

Bode, in the *Jahrbuch der. Kgl. Preuss. Kunstsammlungen*, 1890, vol. XI, p. 207; Dutuit, p. 19;
Michel, pp. 142, 551.

Six Collection, Amsterdam, 1828.
Dʳ Leroy d'Etiolles' collection, Paris, 1861.
M. Ch. Sedelmeyer's collection, Paris, sold at Vienna, 1872.
Posonyi Collection, Vienna.
Herr James Simon's collection, Berlin.

PORTRAIT OF REMBRANDT
IN AN EASTERN DRESS

(KUMS GALLERY, ANTWERP)

PORTRAIT OF REMBRANDT IN AN EASTERN DRESS

(KUMS GALLERY, ANTWERP)

At about the age of twenty-four. Full-face, standing, his gloved left hand on a stick. In a short tunic of a dull copper-red colour, with a broad gold trimming, drawn together with an Oriental scarf. Over this, a dark purple cloak, held back on the hip by the right hand (also gloved), and fastened on the shoulder with three pearl studs. Closely fitting, greenish gray breeches, and high, soft leather boots. Over the long brown curling hair, a high turban of brown and green striped stuff, with a feather. Small moustache. To the left, on a table with a dark bluish-green cover, a helmet, a shawl, and other objects, in chiaroscuro.

Small figure, full-length.
Signed above to the left : *Rembrandt ft. 1641.* (The signature a forgery.)
Painted about 1631-32.

Oak panel. H. 0m,68; w. 0m,50.

Almost a replica of the autograph portrait in M. Dutuit's collection at Rouen.

Smith, n° 299; Dutuit, p. 19.

Lerouge Collection, 1818.
G. Couteaux Collection.
Deuren de Beauprè Collection, 1844
Tardieu Collection, 1851.
Nieuwenhuys (senior) Collection, 1852.
Piérard Collection, 1860.
Kums Gallery, Antwerp. (N° in Catalogue, 130.)

DR. TULP'S ANATOMY-LESSON

(ROYAL GALLERY, THE HAGUE)

DR. TULP'S ANATOMY-LESSON

ROYAL GALLERY, THE HAGUE]

In a vaulted interior, Professor Nicolaes Pietersz Tulp lectures on the anatomy of the muscles of the arm, demonstrating on the corpse of a criminal. He is seated, turned three-quarters to the left, in a black dress, with a plain flat collar and cuffs, and a broad-brimmed hat; he wears a moustache and a small pointed beard. With his uplifted left hand he makes an explanatory gesture, while with the right he holds up the exposed muscles of the left fore-arm with a pair of forceps. The foreshortened corpse, naked but for a white loin-cloth, is laid obliquely on a table. At the feet, in the foreground to the right, lies a great folio volume.

A group of five figures to the right of the lecturer occupies the centre of the picture; two other students sit on the extreme left, in front of the dissecting-table. They are all masters of the Amsterdam Guild of Surgeons. By Tulp's side in the chief group is Mathijs Kalkoen; he bends slightly forward, his face almost full to the specta-tor, his eyes fixed on the speaker, his left hand on his breast. Behind him is Hartman Hartmansz, on a higher bench, his figure in profile to the right, his face turned to the front; in his left hand he holds a paper, on which the names of those present are inscribed. To the right of Kalkoens is Jacob de Witt, bending over to the right, almost in profile, and looking eagerly at the arm of the subject. Leaning over, behind and above him, Jacob Block also watches intently. Behind and above him again on the back seat of the amphitheatre is Frans von Loenen, facing the spectator, his right hand (the left is not seen) grasping the folds of his cloak. To the extreme left of the canvas are Jacob Koolvelt (in profile) and Adriaen Slabran, both seated. The latter turns his face towards the spectator; his right hand rests on his knee. They are all bare-headed; all wear beards and moustaches more or less pro-nounced; all are dressed in black (save de Witt, who wears a dark violet doublet), and all have pleated overhanging collars, with the exception of Hartmansz, who still retains the old-fashioned gauffered ruff.

Half-length figures, life-size.
Signed above in the centre of the canvas (the greater part of the signature has been re-painted) : *Rembrant f. 1632.*

Canvas, H. 1m,6i5; w. 2m,16i.

Etched by J. de Frey, W. Unger, Léopold Flameng, C. Dake ; and twice in aquatint by J. B. A. Cornilliet. — Lithographed by C. Binger, H. J. van den Hout, H. J. Zimmermann, C. C. A. Last, J. L. Huy-gens; and in colour by Lankhout, and Yzerdraad. — Reproduced in Dohme (woodcut); in Woltmann and Woermann; and in Émile Michel's " Rembrandt ". — Drawn by J. Dilhoff in 1760; and by H. Pothoven.
Mentioned by Z. C. van Uffenbach, who visited the Theatrum Anatomicum in 1712 (*Merkwürdige Reisen*, III, p. 576).

Smith, n° 142; Vosmaer, pp. 108, 492; Bode, p. 398, n° 11; Dutuit, p. 36, n° 193; Wurzbach, n° 889; Michel, pp. 131, 565.

Painted for the Surgeon's Guild of Amsterdam, in whose Theatrum Anatomicum the picture remained till 1828.
Royal Gallery, The Hague (since 1828). (N° in Catalogue 317.)

REMBRANDT'S SISTER, WITH A VEIL

(THE BRERA, MILAN)

REMBRANDT'S SISTER, WITH A VEIL

(THE BRERA, MILAN)

Full-face, turned slightly to the left, and looking straight before her. Light red, frizzled hair, from which a veil hangs down behind. Dark dress embroidered with gold; a pleated chemisette at the throat. Dark background. The head strongly illuminated from in front to the left.

Bust, life-size, the hands not seen.

Signed to the right : *R van Ryn 1632*.

Oak panel. Oval. H. 0ᵐ.55: w. 0ᵐ,48.

Engraved by Boutrois; and by Laurent for *Le Musée Français*.

Smith, p. 557; Bode, p. 421, n° 374; Dutuit, p. 47, n° 190; Wurzbach, n° 359; Michel, p. 110, 566.

The Louvre, Paris. 1813; assigned to the Brera, Milan, by Napoleon.
The Brera, Milan. (N° in Catalogue. 449.)

REMBRANDT'S SISTER, FULL-FACE

(LIECHTENSTEIN GALLERY, VIENNA)

REMBRANDT'S SISTER, FULL-FACE

(LIECHTENSTEIN GALLERY, VIENNA)

Facing the spectator, and looking straight before her. She wears a deep purple-red mantle with a broad gold trimming, shewing a pleated chemisette at the throat. Short, curly light red hair; pearl earrings. A strong light falls from above on the face and neck. Grayish background.

Bust, life-size, the hands not seen.
Signed to the right above the shoulder : *RL van Ryn 1632.*

Oak panel. Oval. H. o^m,59; w. o^m,44.

Dutuit, p. 53, n° 189; Michel, pp. 168, 560.

Valpinçon Collection, Paris, 1881.
M. Ch. Sedelmeyer's collection, Paris, 1883.
Secrétan Collection, Paris, 1889.
Liechtenstein Gallery Vienna.

REMBRANDT'S SISTER IN A VELVET CAP

(SIR FRANCIS COOK'S COLLECTION, RICHMOND)

REMBRANDT'S SISTER IN A VELVET CAP

(SIR FRANCIS COOK'S COLLECTION, RICHMOND)

Nearly full-face, slightly to the right, looking straight before her. On her head a dark purple cap with gold braid and a blue feather; a chain in her dark hair. Over her gauze dress she wears a dark mantle, fastened with a gold chain. Round her throat a necklace of pearls divided by small gold balls. Rather a light greenish gray background. A cool, subdued light falls on the head.

Bust, rather less than life-size, the hands not seen.
Signed to the right : *R van Ryn 1632.*

Canvas. Oval. H. 0ᵐ,68; w. 0ᵐ,53.

Lithographed par B... (l. lith. de Villain) under the title : " La Fille de Rembrandt " (sic).

Smith, p. 547; Bode, p. 421, nᵒ 258; Dutuit, pp. 19, 43, nᵒ 186; Wurzbach, nᵒ 168; Michel, pp. 110, 559.

In Smith's time this picture was in a private collection in Paris.
Gentil de Chavagnac Collection, 1854.
Comtesse Lehon's collection, 1861.
Sir Francis Cook's collection, Richmond, Surrey.

REMBRANDT'S SISTER
WITH SMOOTH HAIR

(HERR ALFRED THIEME'S COLLECTION, LEIPZIG)

REMBRANDT'S SISTER, WITH SMOOTH HAIR

Turned slightly to the left, facing the spectator, and looking straight before her. In a black dress lined with gray fur, under which she wears a short greenish brown jacket. The chemisette is open at the throat, shewing a fine gold chain. Her dark hair is combed smoothly back under a little hood of a dull gold colour. The grayish broon background is rather light in tone. The light falls sharply on the head from above, giving great intensity to the shadows.

Bust, nearly life-size, the hands not seen.
Painted about 1642. Unfinished in parts; the hair only laid in.

Oak panel. H. 0ᵐ,56; w. 0ᵐ,42.

Mr. Humphry Ward's collection. London. 1894.
Herr Alfred Thieme's collection, Leipzig.

REMBRANDT'S SISTER
WITH A WIDE LACE COLLAR

(LORD LECONFIELD'S COLLECTION, PETWORTH)

REMBRANDT'S SISTER, WITH A WIDE LACE COLLAR

(LORD LECONFIELD'S COLLECTION, PETWORTH)

Nearly full-face, slightly to the right, looking straight before her. Her fair reddish hair is drawn into a jewelled clasp at the back of her head. A pearl earring in her ear. She wears a flat, closely fitting lace collar over a dark greenish gown with a scarf. A fine gold chain is twisted several times round her neck.

Bust, nearly life-size, the hands not seen.
Pobably painted in 1632, with the pendant n° 61.

Oak panel. Oval. H. 0^m,63; w. 0^m,48.

A companion picture to the Portrait of Rembrandt, dated 1632 (Plate 61).
Etched with the above on the same plate by Ingouf the younger for the " Galerie du Palais-Royal ", Paris, 1786-1809.

Bode, p. 421, n° 252; Dutuit, p. 46, n° 187; Wurzbach, n° 216; Michel, pp. 110, 559.

Duc d'Orléans' collection, Palais-Royal.
Lord Leconfield's collection, Petworth.

PORTRAIT OF REMBRANDT

(LORD LECONFIELD'S COLLECTION, PETWORTH)

PORTRAIT OF REMBRANDT

LORD LECONFIELD'S COLLECTION, PETWORTH

Nearly full-face, looking straight before him, a black hat on his dark frizzled hair. He wears a black doublet with yellow buttons, over which hangs a white pleated collar. Light background. Strongly illuminated from the left.

Bust, nearly life-size, the hands not seen.
Signed to the right : *Re van Ryn 1632.*

Oak panel. Oval. H. o^m,64; w, o^m,48.

Companion picture to the Portrait of Rembrandt' Sister (Plate 60), with which it was etched on the same plate by Ingouf (Cf. n° 60).

Bode, p. 591 ; Dutuit, p. 46; Wurzbach, n° 214; Michel, pp. 100, 559.

Lord Leconfield's collection. Petworth.

REMBRANDT'S SISTER
IN A RICHLY EMBROIDERED BODICE

(THE MARQUISE DE CARCANO'S COLLECTION, PARIS)

REMBRANDT'S SISTER

IN A RICHLY EMBROIDERED BODICE

THE MARQUISE DE CARCANO'S COLLECTION, PARIS

Slightly to the right, her head turned to the spectator. Light red frizzled hair, a pearl earring in her ear. The black bodice, richly embroidered with gold, displays a simple white collar at the throat. Strongly illuminated from the left.

Bust, life-size, the hands not seen.
Painted about 1632.

Oak panel. Oval. H. 0m,52; w, 0m,39

This portrait has more in common with the example in the Liechtenstein Gallery than with any other of the series.

Etched by Bracquemond in outline for the Demidoff sale catalogue.

Smith IX. n° 15; Vosmaer, p. 500; Dutuit, p. 51, n° 191; Wurzbach, n° 296.

Sold in London, about 1800.
Van Nagell van Ampsen Collection, The Hague, 1851.
Prince Anatole Demidoff's collection. San Donato: sold in Paris in 1868.
Marquise de Carcano's collection, Paris.

REMBRANDT'S SISTER, IN PROFILE

(NATIONAL MUSEUM, STOCKHOLM)

REMBRANDT'S SISTER, IN PROFILE

To the left, standing, in profile, the left hand concealed, the right gloved, and holding a feather fan with a golden handle. The brownish red velvet mantle bordered with gold embroidery is fastened across the breast with a large gold clasp. The daintily pleated chemisette is held round the throat by a string of pearls. A large pearl in the ear. The light reddish hair is gathered into a net, fastened with a jewelled clasp, through which a knot of flowers is thrust.

Half length, life-size.
Signed above the shoulder to the right : *Rt van Ryn 1632.*

Canvas. H. 0ᵐ.71; w. 0ᵐ.74.

Etched (reversed) by W. de Leeuw (Bartsch, II, p. 132, n° 47; Bartsch erroneously gives the picture in the Cassel Gallery, then in the De Renver Collection at Delft, as the original of this plate).

Mr. Alexander, of London, owns an exact replica (see Plate 64), and Mrs. Alfred Seymour, of London, a school copy of the head.

Smith, n° 571; Vosmaer, p. 494; Bode, p. 417, n° 364; Dutuit, p. 40, n° 179; Wurzbach, n° 439; Michel, pp. 168, 568.

K. G. Tessin Collection.
Queen Louisa Ulrica's collection, Sweden.
National Museum, Stockholm. (N° in Catalogue 583.)

REMBRANDT'S SISTER, IN PROFILE

(MR. WILLIAM C. ALEXANDER'S COLLECTION, LONDON)

REMBRANDT'S SISTER, IN PROFILE

(MR. WILLIAM C. ALEXANDER'S COLLECTION, LONDON)

Standing, in profile, to the left. In a reddish brown mantle with trimmings of gold brocade, holding a fan with a gilded handle in her right hand, on which is a fur glove. The deep violet dress shews the chemisette at the throat, round which it is held by a string of pearls. A pearl in the ear. The light red hair is arranged in a knot at the back of the head, bound by a greenish blue ribbon fastened with a richly set ruby. A spray of flowers is thrust through the ribbon. Dark background.

Half-length, life-size.
Painted about 1632.

Canvas, to which a strip has been added all round. H. 0ᵐ,68; w. 0ᵐ,5x.

An exact replica of the signed picture in the Stockholm Gallery (Plate 63).
Mrs. Seymour, of London, owns a school copy of the head.

Earl of Denbigh's collection, Newnham Paddox, 1894.
Mr. William C. Alexander's collection, London.

REMBRANDT'S SISTER
IN A FUR-TRIMMED CLOAK

(BARONESS HIRSCH DE GEREUTH'S COLLECTION, PARIS)

REMBRANDT'S SISTER IN A FUR-TRIMMED CLOAK

BARONESS HIRSCH DE GEREUTH'S COLLECTION, PARIS)

Slightly to the left, the face full to the spectator, looking straight before her. Light red hair, a pearl in the ear. The dark fur-trimmed cloak is fastened across the breast with a gold clasp, but shews a gold chain beneath, and the white chemisette above. Dark background. Strong light from the left.

Bust, life-size, the hands not seen.
Signed below to the right : *R van Ryn 1633.*

Canvas. Oval. H. 0m,57; w. 0m,43.

Smith, n° 499, or 500; Vosmaer, p. 495; Michel, pp. 173, 563.

Julienne Collection, Paris, 1767.
Rochard Collection, Paris, 1858.
A. Roehn Collection, Paris, 1868.
M. Ch. Sedelmeyer's collection, Paris, 1869.
Mrs. Brooks' collection, Paris, 1877.
Baroness Hirsch de Gereuth's collection, Paris.

REMBRANDT'S SISTER
WITH A GOLD CHAIN

(M. A. POLOWTSOFF'S COLLECTION, ST. PETERSBURG)

REMBRANDT'S SISTER WITH A GOLD CHAIN

(M. A. POLOWTSOFF'S COLLECTION, ST. PETERSBURG)

Standing, to the left, her head slightly inclined, and turned to the spectator. She wears a purple-red, fur-lined mantle, over a pale blue bodice, cut low, and shewing the edge of the chemisette and a pearl necklace. A triple gold chain hangs across her breast. The fair, reddish hair, waves in little curls, and is adorned in front with rubies, and behind with a pearl embroidered veil, which hangs down her back. Dark background. The light falls full on the head from above.

Bust, life-size, the hands not seen.
Signed below to the left : *Rembrandt f. 1633*.

Canvas. H. 0m,730; w. 0m,635.

Mr. Massey Mainwaring's collection, London, 1892.
Mr. Charles J. Wertheimer's collection, 1894.
M. A. Polowtsoff's collection, St. Petersburg.

MINERVA
ABSORBED IN THE STUDY OF A BOOK

(M. POL-CHARBONNEAU'S COLLECTION, REIMS)

MINERVA ABSORBED IN THE STUDY OF A BOOK

(M. POL-CHARBONNEAUX'S COLLECTION, REIMS)

Seated, absorbed in the study of a book, to the left, at a round table, with a greenish blue cover bordered with gold. In a violet dress, partly covered by a purple mantle embroidered with gold, which is laid over the chair behind her. On the table a book, a lute, an Oriental shawl, etc. On a shelf behind her to the right, books and a globe. A shield with the Gorgon's head hangs upon a dull violet banner, against an imbedded column of the wall. The abundant brown hair is drawn back from the somewhat forbidding young face, and confined by a gold circlet. The light comes from the left, and falls beyond the figure.

Small figure, full-length.
Painted about 1631.

Oak panel. H. 0ᵐ,435; w. 0ᵐ,350.

M. Ch. Sedelmeyer's collection, Paris, 1896.
M. Pol-Charbonneaux's collection, Reims.

MINERVA

(ROYAL GALLERY, BERLIN)

MINERVA

(ROYAL GALLERY, BERLIN)

A young woman, seated to the left, in the foreground of a room, at a table on which lie folios, a lute and a coat of mail. She turns to face the spectator, dressed in a bluish green robe brocaded with silver; over it a deep purple red mantle with a gold border, which conceals her arms. On her flowing fair hair lies a crown of laurel, in which a small upright twig is fastened. On the wall a trophy, composed of a shield with a Medusa's head, a sword and a helmet.

Small figure, full-length.
On the right, about half way up the panel, traces of the monogram.
Painted about 1632.
Much faded and cracked by long exposure to the sun.

Oak panel. H. 0ᵐ,59; w. 0ᵐ,48.

Bode, p. 388, n° 72; Dutuit, p. 25, n° 71; Wurzbach, n° 29; Michel, pp. 107, 551.

Formerly in the Royal Palace, Berlin, as " Minerva ", by Rembrandt; probably one of the pictures inherited from Princess Amelia of Solms († 1675).

Royal Gallery, Berlin. N° in Catalogue, 828°). At the opening of the museum in 1830 it was pronounced the work of Ferdinand Bol, and was soon afterwards relegated to the magazine; reinstated in 1880, and restored to its rightful author.

REMBRANDT'S SISTER AT HER TOILET
(THE SO-CALLED JEWISH BRIDE)

(LIECHTENSTEIN GALLERY, VIENNA)

REMBRANDT'S SISTER AT HER TOILET
(THE SO-CALLED JEWISH BRIDE)

LIECHTENSTEIN GALLERY, VIENNA

Seated in the foreground, slightly to the right, facing the spectator; in a sleeveless robe of a strong brownish red tone, lined with golden yellow, and trimmed with a wide gold border, over an under-dress of pale violet embroidered with gold. Full gauze sleeves, with gold embroideries. A clasp and a pale blue feather fastened into her flowing hair, which an old woman in a dull green dress behind her is about to comb. Behind the group, a table with silver vessels, jewellery, books, etc., against a dull violet curtain. Against the wall to the right, which is divided by pilasters, stands a cushioned seat.

Small figures, full-length.
Signed below, in the middle, on the step : *Rembrant f. 1632.*

Canvas. H. 1m,08 : w; 0m,91.

There is a sketch for this picture in the Albertina, Vienna. n° 909.
Exhibited at the British Gallery, 1818.

Smith, n° 494; Vosmaer, p. 495; Dutuit, p. 15, n° 366; Michel, pp. 169, 560.

Madame de Bandeville's collection, 1787.
Lord Rendlesham's collection, 1806.
Earl of Mulgrave's collection, 1832.
Mr. Seguier's collection.
Sir W. W. Knighton's collection, 1885.
Sir Charles Robinson's collection, London, 1888.
M. Ch. Sedelmeyer's collection, 1890.
Liechtenstein Gallery, Vienna.

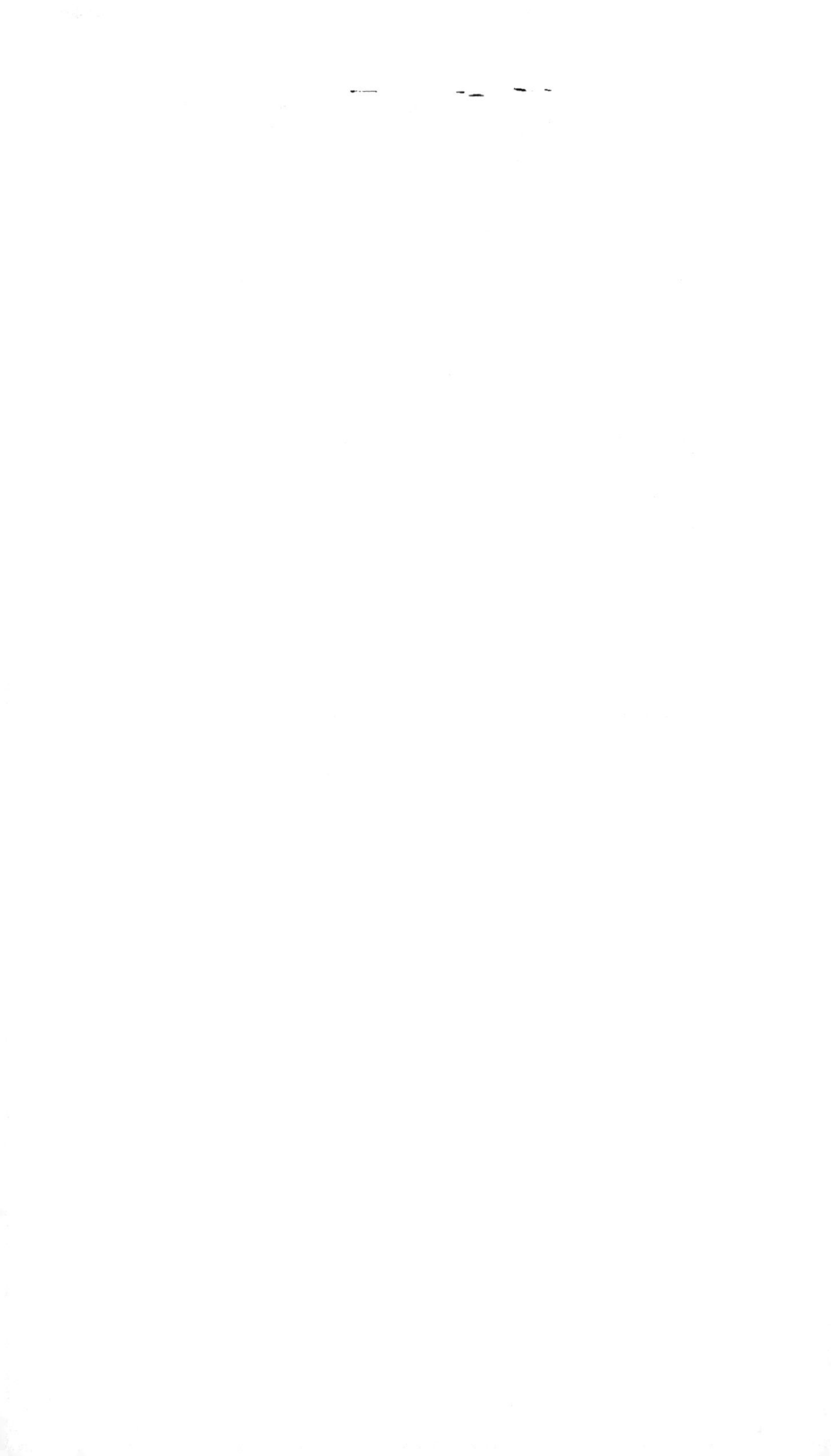

THE RAPE OF PROSERPINE

(ROYAL GALLERY, BERLIN

THE RAPE OF PROSERPINE

(ROYAL GALLERY, BERLIN)

Pluto, in his chariot, holding the captive Proserpine in his arms, is about to plunge into the waters to the right. Three richly caparisoned black horses draw the fantastic chariot, covered with plaques of gold, and ornamented in front with the mask of a roaring lion. Pluto guides the team with a chain; a gold-embroidered brown mantle is thrown over his naked limbs; both his arms are round the princess, who, in her despair, attacks his face with her hands. Over her light silken robe she wears a white mantle worked with gold, and, in her fair hair, a handful of flowers. The basket of flowers she was carrying falls from the chariot on the left. Two of her companions, in pale violet and lilac dresses, one carrying a quiver on her back, cling to their mistress' mantle to rescue her, but are dragged along the flowery meadow by the fiery onward rush of the chariot.

Thistle and lotos plants grow along the shore in the foreground to the left; to the right rises a steep bank with a palisade.

Small figures, full-length.
Painted about 1632.

Oak panel. H. 0m,83; w. 0m,78.

Vosmaer, pp. 117, 492; Bode, p. 438, n° 31; Dutuit, p. 25, n° 105; Wurzbach, n° 16; Michel, pp. 107, 551.

Inherited in 1676 by the Great Elector from the Princess Amelia of Solms, widow of the Stadholder Frederick Henry of Orange.

Royal Palace, Berlin.

Royal Gallery, Berlin. N° in Catalogue 823.¹ Formerly ascribed, in the Catalogue, to the etcher, Jan Joris van Vliet, but rightly assigned to Rembrandt as long as it remained in the Palace.

THE RAPE OF EUROPA

(COLLECTION OF THE PRINCESSE DE BROGLIE, NÉE SAY, PARIS)

In the foreground to the left, Jupiter, in the form of a white bull, has plunged into the water, carrying Europa upon his back. The princess clings to him with both hands, and gazes back despairingly at her companions, who look on in great alarm. One is seated, a second stands beside her, in pofile; a third is in the road, in front of a chariot with four white horses, in which is a large sunshade. The driver, a Moor, has risen, and looks after the bull in amazement. In the distance to the left, a sea-port town, with domes and flat towers; in front stands a tower with a crane, approached by a bridge, near which lie several boats. Pale blue sky with floating clouds.

The rich, fantastic dresses of the women are purple-red, greenish blue, violet, and brown, with wide gold borders. They wear veils and gold chains.

Small figures, full-length.
Signed *Rembrant f. 1632.*

Oak panel. H. o^m,6o; w. o^m,77.

Cf. P. Lacroix *Annuaire des Artistes,* 1862.
Smith, n° 188; Vosmaer, pp. 117, 192; Bode, p. 438. Dutuit. p. 20; Wurzbach, n° 306; Michel,
p. 108.

Comtesse de Verrue's collection, 1737 (?) (Smith, n° 188; ascribed to Eeckhout).
Duc de Morny's collection. Paris, 1865.
Collection of the Princesse de Broglie, née Say, Paris.

CONTENTS OF VOLUME I

Preface   I

INTRODUCTION

I. Rembrandt's youthful Works. Period of activity in his native city, Leyden, 1627 to 1631. . . .   1
II. The removal to Amsterdam. The Anatomy-Lesson; Autograph Portraits, and Portraits of the Artist's Sister, Lysbeth Harmens, of the year 1632   23

CATALOGUE OF REMBRANDT'S PICTURES, PART I

1. The Money-Changer. (Berlin Museum)   35
2. St. Paul in Prison. (Royal Museum, Stuttgart)   37
3. St. Paul, by Candlelight. (Germanic Museum, Nuremberg).   39
4. A Savant studying by Candlelight. (Madame Mayer's collection, Vienna).   41
5. St. Peter among the Servants of the High Priest. (Herr Karl von der Heydt's collection, Berlin) .   43
6. Samson captured by the Philistines. (Royal Palace, Berlin).   45
7. The Presentation of Christ in the Temple. (Herr Ed. F. Weber's collection, Hamburg). . . .   47
8. An old Man asleep by the Fire. (Royal Gallery, Turin).   49
9. The Supper at Emmaus. (Madame Édouard André's collection, Paris).   51
10. Judas bringing back the thirty Pieces of Silver. (Baron Schickler's collection, Paris). . . .   53
11. Rembrandt with disordered Hair. (Royal Gallery, Cassel).   55
12. Rembrandt (?) laughing. (Royal Gallery, The Hague)   57
13. Rembrandt gazing enquiringly at the Spectator. (Ducal Museum, Gotha).   59
14. Rembrandt with a black Cap. (Signor Ferdinando Meazza's collection, Milan).   61
15. Rembrandt laughing, with a Cap on the back of his Head. (M. Henri Heugel's collection, Paris) .   63
16. Rembrandt with a Steel Gorget. (Royal Gallery, The Hague).   65
17. Rembrandt in a Morning Gown. (Count Julius Andrassy's collection, Buda-Pesth). . . .   67
18. Rembrandt in a plumed Cap. (Mrs. John L. Gardner's collection, Boston)   69
19. Portrait of Rembrandt's Mother. Small Size. (Dr. A. Bredius' collection, The Hague) .   71
20. Rembrandt's Father as " Philo the Jew ". (Ferdinandeum, Innsbruck)   73
21. Rembrandt's Mother in a black Hood. (Mr. Arthur Sanderson's collection, Edinburgh). . .   75
22. Rembrandt's Mother reading. (Earl of Pembroke's collection, Wilton House) . . .   77
23. Rembrandt's Mother as the Prophetess Anna. (Grand-Ducal Gallery, Oldenburg).   79
24. Rembrandt's Mother with a large Head-Covering. (H. M. the Queen's collection, Windsor Castle).   81
25. Rembrandt's Father gazing fixedly at the Spectator. (Dr. Melville Wassermann's collection, Paris).   83
26. Rembrandt's Father. Small Size. (Municipal Museum, Vienna)   85
27. Rembrandt's Father in a plumed Cap. (The Hermitage, St. Petersburg)   87
28. Rembrandt's Father in a Cap with a blue Feather. (Mr. W. B. Chamberlin's collection, Brighton).   89
29. Rembrandt's Father in a broad-brimmed Hat. (Mr. W. A. Beers' collection, New York). . . .   91
30. Rembrandt's Father in a Fur Cloak. (Dr. A. Bredius' collection, The Hague) . . .   93

31. Rembrandt's Father in a Morning Gown. (Royal Gallery, Cassel) 95
32. An old Man, with a gold Cross on his Breast. (Royal Gallery, Cassel). 97
33. Portrait of an old Man, with a bristly Beard. (Signor E. P. Fabbri's collection, Florence) . 99
34. St. Paul writing his Epistle to the Thessalonians. (M. J. H. Harjes' collection, Paris. . 101
35. St. Paul seated at a Writing-Table and meditating. (Imperial Gallery, Vienna). 103
36. St. Paul seated at a Writing-Table and meditating. (Mr. M. C. D. Borden's collection, New York). 105
37. The Holy Family resting during the Flight into Egypt. (Mr. A. R. Boughton Knight's collection, Downton Castle). 107
38. The Holy Family in the Carpenter's Shop. (Royal Pinacothek, Munich) 109
39. Jeremiah mourning the Destruction of Jerusalem. (Count Sergei Stroganoff's collection, St. Petersburg). 111
40. St. Anastasius. (National Museum, Stockholm). 113
41. St. Peter penitent. (Prince de Rubempré de Mérode's collection, Brussels). 115
42. High Priest with a Book. (M. Albert Lehmann's collection, Paris). . 117
43. The Savant. (Ducal Gallery, Brunswick) 119
44. Simeon in the Temple. (Royal Gallery, The Hague) 121
45. The Raising of Lazarus. (Mr. Ch. T. Yerkes' collection, New York). 123
46. David playing the Harp before Saul. (Staedel Institute, Frankfort). 125
47. Diana bathing. (Mr. E. Warneck's collection, Paris). 127
48. Portrait of a young Lad. (Herr Adolph Thiem's collection, San Remo) 129
49. A young Man in a Turban. (Windsor Castle). 131
50. Portrait of a Savant (The so-called Portrait of Coppenol). (The Hermitage, St. Petersburg). . 133
51. Portrait of Nicolas Ruts. (Mr. Jos. Ruston's collection, Lincoln) 135
52. Portrait of a young Girl. (Dr. A. Bredius' collection, The Hague) 137
53. A young Girl, standing in an Interior. (Herr James Simon's collection, Berlin). . 139
54. Portrait of Rembrandt in an Eastern Dress. (Kunst Gallery, Antwerp). . . . 141
55. Dr. Tulp's Anatomy-Lesson. (Royal Gallery, The Hague) 143
56. Rembrandt's Sister, with a Veil. (The Brera, Milan) 145
57. Rembrandt's Sister, full-face. (Liechtenstein Gallery, Vienna). 147
58. Rembrandt's Sister in a velvet Cap. (Sir Francis Cook's collection, Richmond) . 149
59. Rembrandt's Sister with smooth Hair. (Herr Alfred Thieme's collection, Leipzig) . 151
60. Rembrandt's Sister with a wide Lace Collar. (Lord Leconfield's collection, Petworth). . . 153
61. Portrait of Rembrandt. (Lord Leconfield's collection, Petworth) 155
62. Rembrandt's Sister in a richly embroidered Bodice. (The Marquise de Carcano's collection, Paris). 157
63. Rembrandt's Sister, in Profile. (National Museum, Stockholm) 159
64. Rembrandt's Sister, in Profile. (Mr. William C. Alexander's collection, London). 161
65. Rembrandt's Sister in a fur-trimmed Cloak. (Baroness Hirsch de Gereuth's collection, Paris). 163
66. Rembrandt's Sister with a gold Chain. (M. Polowtsoff's collection, St. Petersburg) . . 165
67. Minerva absorbed in the Study of a Book. (M. Pol-Charbonneaux's collection, Rheims). 167
68. Minerva. (Royal Gallery, Berlin). 169
69. Rembrandt's Sister at her Toilet (the so-called Jewish Bride) (Liechtenstein Gallery, Vienna). 171
70. The Rape of Proserpine. (Royal Gallery, Berlin) 173
71. The Rape of Europa. (Collection of the Princesse de Broglie, née Say, Paris) 175